CW00498442

In Search of Re
The First Deca.... ... ...
Soviet State

by R H Haigh
D S Morris
and A R Peters

Sheffield Hallam University Press
Learning Centre
City Campus
Pond Street
Sheffield S1 1WB

Designed and typeset by Design Studio, Learning Centre,
Sheffield Hallam University

All rights reserved. No part of this publication may be
reproduced, stored in a retrieval system, or transmitted in
any form or by any means, electronic, mechanical,
photocopying, recording, or otherwise, without prior written
permission of the publishers.

©2003   ISBN 0 86339 980 0

 *Sheffield Hallam University*

Contents Page

Chapter One

Explanations of Soviet Foreign Policy

The analysis of governmental policy, be it in the field of domestic or foreign policy, is not an activity which is explicable simply in terms of cause and consequence. As a human activity, policy-making reflects all of the frailties of human reasoning and rarely is it possible to depict, with any degree of comprehensiveness, the motivations and calculations which underlie the formulation, implementation and effect of a particular policy; nor is it generally possible to discern a sequentially logical pattern to policy issues in any single policy field. The inability of the policy-maker to have at his disposal an exhaustive list of relevant factors, a total understanding of those factors, and an appreciation of their intended consequences, to say nothing of those consequences which are unintended, as well as the subjective preferences, prejudices and motivations of the policy-maker, all ensure that total rationality can never be reflected in any particular policy.[1] The study of policy thus becomes something far less than a scientifically accurate undertaking, dealing as it does, with a subject matter which is itself the product of human activity. In consequence, the policy analyst is constantly obliged to have recourse to interpretation and, on occasions, to fall back on supposition and the playing of more or less well substantiated hunches. All of this is by way of contending that policy analysis is an area of endeavour in which difficulties abound; but it is not intended to imply that the task should not be attempted, nor that any conclusions which may emerge are so open to question as to make them invalid, nor pitched at such a high level of generality as to render them meaningless.

These problems, it must be emphasised, are an ever-present hurdle to any analysis of any policy, they are not the peculiar reserve of a particular policy nor are they confined to a particular policy area; they are as cogent to the study of domestic policy as they are to the study of foreign policy. Yet, if anything, they are perhaps of greater magnitude in the case of the latter than they are in the case of the former, for foreign policy is used by governments not simply to secure the support of their own nationals but also the support of the governments and nationals of other sovereign states. In consequence, foreign policy frequently carries an element of generality and flexibility which is of less import in domestic policy as the response at a nation's foreign policy is likely to elicit in other governments is less capable of accurate prediction than the response which a government can expect from its own citizens to its domestic policy; if for no other reason than that different nations have different traditions, cultures, histories etc. Then the foreign policy under analysis was that of the Soviet Union additional problems were present over and above those so far discerned; problems which owe their origin to the nature of the internal organisation of the Soviet state. Foremost among these was the consideration that political leadership of the USSR exercises what amounted to virtually total control over the sources of information both within, and emanating from, their country:

> "... in the Soviet Union the press is a governmental agency; there is no free public discussion of international issues, no open debate between competing leadership groups. Policies are determined in secret by means unknown to us ... retired Soviet diplomats do not publish memoirs. And though Soviet diplomatic documents are being published, too often they are edited to present the official 'line' of the moment rather than to reveal the truth about the events described"[2]

The fact that the USSR was governed by a single, monolithic political party with a highly structured ideological component embracing much more than simply the national goals of the Soviet Union but also encompassing the wider goals of the international communist movement, and Soviet leadership of that movement, implied a duality in the foreign policy of the USSR which can thus be said to reflect not merely the national aims and objectives of the Soviet state per se but also the goals of the USSR as the leader of the national communist movement.

Given the difficulties entailed, it is hardly surprising that a number of explanations have been advanced in search of the key which would permit an understanding of Soviet foreign policy to be gained and clarification of Soviet intentions to be acquired:

"The study of Soviet politics, and especially of Soviet foreign policy, has ... been characterised by (the) search for a skeleton key which used by itself might explain motivation and resultant action by the Soviet Union in the international system".[3]

From the range of explanations offered of Soviet foreign policy it is worthwhile considering some of the more commonly advanced which can be considered under a number of rather broad headings:

a) **Geopolitical.** Although it suffered a fall in support compared with that which it enjoyed in the 1940s this school of thought contended that Soviet foreign policy was largely a direct result of the opportunities and limitations imposed by the USSRs position as a great land mass. Kerner argued that Russia and, later, Soviet foreign policy had been formulated by the constant need to secure routes to the open sea along its borders for, without the control of such routes, her independence could be readily threatened by other nations restricting her trade and freedom of movement. Kerner maintained that a study of Tsarist Russia revealed a perpetual pattern of disputes with neighboring countries over the control of sea ports and access to them, and that Soviet foreign policy basically reflected a continuation of this dispute.[4] Cressey presented views not dissimilar to those of Kerner:

"The history of Russia may be written in terms of its search for ocean ports. The Russian Bear will not be content until it finds warm water, and this is equally true regardless of whether the government be a czarist autarchy or Soviet Socialism."[5]

Cressey's adherence to this view, however, was gradually modified and he later came to make concessions to the role of other factors influencing Soviet motivations, such as ideological and economic considerations, whilst still holding that the geographical position of the USSR acted as the fundamental catalyst to other motives; especially Soviet security needs.[6]

Among other writers in the geopolitical school agreement was not always so readily apparent, as was revealed by the differing interpretations of the motives behind Soviet foreign policy produced by Strausz-Hupe and Vernadsky. For Strausz-Hupe the foreign policy of both Tsarist and Soviet Russia had been primarily formulated out of a consideration to make secure her geographically vulnerable western frontiers, and that Soviet designs in the east only received attention when her attempts in the west had been frustrated.[7] Opposing such a view is that of Vernadsky. For Vernadsky the foreign policy of both Tsarist and Soviet Russia had shown a concentration upon the possibility of eastward expansion because of the absence of any geographical barriers in that direction.[8]"

Those accounts, and others adopting a geopolitical interpretation, were heavily deterministic in character implying that the freedom of maneuver open to Soviet foreign policy-makers was constrained or severely curtailed as a result of the geographical characteristics of the Soviet nation; and whilst such factors had no doubt played a part in the formulation of Soviet foreign policy it was highly questionable whether they had ever exclusively provided the motivation behind that policy or whether they have remained unchanging in their importance and impact upon Soviet foreign policy throughout the years; particularly in the face of technological advances and the changes in the strategic possibilities which these heralded.

b) **Cultural and Personality**. Here the focus had been on seeking an explanation of Soviet foreign policy on the basis of Soviet behaviour with national character providing the focal concept. The contention of this school of thought was summarised by Bell:

> *"The argument is that members of a given culture share certain common, sufficiently distinct ways of handling emotional drives and regulating social conduct which form a unique life style that differs, often markedly, from the life style of other cultural groups. The 'norms' of the group specify how an individual must manage the key tensions generated in social living..."*[9]

The approach was derived from social anthropology and presented two real problem areas; namely, to what extent could there be said to be a national character, implying as it did a very high degree of uniformity among people of the same nation; and what was the relationship of national character, assuming it could be accurately portrayed and substantiated, and the motivations behind Soviet foreign policy? With these considerations in mind, and remembering that emphasis has been placed on the "Great Russian character", it is possible to briefly detail the work of some of the foremost advocates of the culture and personality school. Gorer and Rickman contend that the practice of tightly swaddling the Russian infant initiates a privation-gratification cycle founded upon a total restriction-total freedom dichotomy which results in the "Great Russian" national character having a predisposition to swing between submissiveness and violent outbursts, from apathy to anxiety. On the basis of this observation, Gorer and Rickman produce several "political maxims" for Soviet behaviour.[10] Rosser notes the following as being of particular relevance to an understanding of Soviet foreign policy:

> "... suspicion by both the elite and the masses of the outside world springs from unconscious and thus irrational sources, and cannot be eliminated through rational action by outsiders; both the elite and the masses feel the need to continually expand their national boundaries until met by superior force; when superior force is met, strategic retreat is a highly acceptable manoeuvre and not humiliating because as Russians they have pushed outward to their utmost ability; attempts to persuade the Russians to admit error in their ideology are futile because admitting one error destroys the whole system of truth, and consequently Russian self-esteem is destroyed."[11]

Dicks, in the emphasis he place on the ambivalence of the Soviet character, is on common ground with Gorer and Rickman, but he goes on to point out a distinction between the national character of the elite and that of the masses.[12]

> "Against the traditional untidiness, lack of system, and formlessness of the Russian masses is the

contrasting behaviour of the elite. It has to be
puritanical, in full control of all sentimentality and
self indulgence, and strong enough to renounce the
gratifications which 'traditional' Russian character
seeks."[13]

Although Dicks argues that both character types are
to be found in the Soviet Union there do exist
congruities between them,

"The people expect and the elite satisfies the image of
authority as severe, arbitrary, and fickle".[14]

The relevance of Dicks' work to the analysis of
Soviet foreign policy is, perhaps, best described as
"tangential". There is, however, some relevance in his
suggestion that,

"... the elite, facing intense inner conflict in the
society because of the pressing need to produce a new
managerial and technological class, have projected
any failures onto 'foreign out-groups' ... which
'encircle' the USSR".

Leites offers a psychoanalytical attempt to discern
the Soviet character based upon the application of
psychoanalytical techniques to the writings of Lenin
and Stalin, and arrives at the conclusion that Bolshevik
behaviour, characterised by rigidity, suspicion and
being unyielding and perpetually aggressive, stems
from Lenin's unconscious reaction to the behaviour of
the nineteenth-century Russian intelligentsia; whom
Leites portrays as moody, nervous, introspective, and
indecisive.[16]In counter-position to the behaviour
pattern of the nineteenth century Russian personality
there is held to emerge the Bolshevik certainty of

purpose and commitment to action reflected in the preparedness to work and in service to the party. From such an investigation came the Bolshevik "operational code" for political action, since politics is determined by action, which Leites summarises as ktokovo; literally translated "who-whom", but, in reality, "who gets whom". From this formula was derived the rules of the political game comprising maxims such as awaiting the opportune moment for action, acting only when fully prepared, refusing to respond to provocation. At least one political consequence of this for Soviet foreign policy was the realisation that peaceful co-existence between the Soviet Union and the western world was, at best, a temporary situation and not one capable of becoming permanent:

> "A 'settlement' in Western terms, with outside groups - an agreement sharply and indefinitely reducing the threat of mutual annihilation - is inconceivable, ... agreements ... codifying the momentary relationship of forces, must be considered and often concluded".[17]

For reasons already suggested the relevance of these approaches to the understanding of Soviet foreign policy remained questionable.

It might have been asked why not study the behaviour of the Soviet foreign policy-makers at first hand rather than trying to discern the motives initiating that behaviour on the basis of highly generalised assessments, not of the policy-makers' characters, but of those of an invariably contentiously derived sample of their fellow countrymen; and, in Leites' case, the writings of but two of them, both dead.

c) **Historical.** Those who argued the theme of "eternal Russia" have enjoyed a respectable longevity. Their thesis was that historical patterns and traditions had an important impact upon the then contemporary Soviet behaviour. Whilst, perhaps not always going so far as to explicitly state that the past determines the present, members of this school of thought have found it an irresistible temptation to point to the "influence" that the past still exerted upon the present. Changes in the social and political structure of the Soviet Union in the 1980s, and in its foreign policy, were, it is contended, more superficial than they would at first sight appear; for underlying them was the bedrock of historical precedent. Certainly such a view was given a good airing in the works of Berdyaev.[18] The similarities that Berdyaev drew between Bolshevik Russia on the one hand and Muscovite Tsardom and the empire of Peter the Great on the other were well sketched by Rosser:

> *(Berdyaev) saw 'Bolshevism' as the third appearance of Russian autocratic imperialism ... Bolshevism stood for a strong centralised and militarised state, but so had old Russia. Bolshevism instituted a dictatorship, similar to the ruling pattern of the Tsars ... "and made use of the characteristics of the Russian mind - its religious instinct and dogmatism, its search for social justice, its messianism and faith in Russia's own path of development. Bolshevism was successful because it was more fruitful to certain Russian 'primordial' traditions than other prescriptions for reform."[19]*

To argue that one political regime might possess some of the features of those which have preceded it is acceptable, provided that this is not taken to the lengths of suggesting that the political institutions and political processes of the new regime are simply the product of past events. Also it is questionable to attribute similar motives to decisions which, judged by their outward manifestation, appear to be similar. It would not, be unreasonable to contend, for example, that Soviet expansionism was motivated by very different considerations to those underlying Tsarist expansionism whilst at the same time agreeing that outwardly both have taken not dissimilar paths. Whilst it is also acceptable to hold that the leaders of the Soviet Union in the early 1980s did not, and indeed could not ignore the history of their country when formulating both its domestic and foreign policy, it another matter altogether to assume that past events in Soviet national life determine the policy decisions arrived at then. Policy is always the subject of constraints, but that it is not to argue that the constraints are unchanging, nor that the scope of action within relatively persistent constraints is not capable of extension.

d) **Totalitarianism**. Adherents to this interpretation of Soviet foreign policy contended that a radically new social form, different from authoritarian regimes of the past and also differing from tyranny and dictatorships in that it sought to control all aspects of societal life, was created in Nazi Germany and flourished in the Soviet Union. That new social form contained a unique feature which, as much as anything, distinguished it from other types of regime; namely that all secondary associations between the political leadership and the mass of the populace had been either eliminated or placed under centralised state directive and, in consequence, the leadership was unconstrained by legal and political checks upon its power. The analysts of totalitarianism reached a fair degree of consensus about the relationship which existed between such a political system and the foreign policy which emanated from it. There was claimed to be little probability of major change in the nature of the totalitarian regime and that the inner momentum of totalitarianism was inherently expansionist and aggressive, thus ensuring that its overt opposition to democratic regimes was unlikely to be modified; although, as Rosser noted:

> "... these (totalitarian) analysts are not exactly sure how this aggressiveness fits into the totalitarian system."[20]

This was apparent in the work of Friedrich and Brzezinski who, whilst portraying the totalitarian regime as were characterised by a number of interrelated features; namely, an ideology, a single party, a centrally directed economy, a monopoly of the communications media, use of force, and a terroristic police, did not go so far as to show how these features related to an aggressive and expansionist foreign policy whilst at the same time making no secret of the fact that totalitarian foreign policy exhibits both such features, referring as they did to:

> "... the struggle for world conquest which is the totalitarian's natural bent..."[21]

and also intimating strongly a direct relationship between totalitarianism and foreign policy,

"... the will to conquer the world which is intimately linked with their ideological preoccupations ... is the outward thrust of that 'passion for unanimity' which brooks no disagreement with what the movement has proclaimed 'as the truth'."[22]

Arendt offered a not dissimilar interpretation of Soviet foreign policy in that the starting point was again totalitarianism.[23] Arendt held that the totalitarian leadership was seeking to exert total control over the individual and was obliged to create a fictitious world based on the myths of the totalitarian movement as a means to that end, since failure to do so would make such control of the individual impossible to achieve. The creation and maintenance of that fictitious world was, however, rendered extremely difficult if factual information was available in the totalitarian state for, virtually by definition, this factual information highlighted the fictitious nature of the totalitarian world. To prevent this eventuality arising, and the consequent loss of power that the leadership would have over the totalitarian society, it was necessary for the totalitarian state to eliminate the source of such factual information; a task which could only be achieved by world conquest. Hence, the attempt to secure world domination was an inherent part of the totalitarian system. Clearly there were problems with such an interpretation of Soviet foreign policy. Firstly, it was questionable whether or not the Soviet Union was actually a totalitarian regime when there was evidence to suggest that there existed competition between factions for the leadership function, and also that accommodation had to be made by the leadership to strategically located groups within the society, such as military and economic interests. Foreign policy can be said to be nothing more than one output from this political process, and as Rosser noted was:

"... hardly the single-minded pursuit of one dictator for total world control."[24]

Secondly, even if it is accepted that the Soviet Union was a totalitarian regime, and even if it is conceded that the Soviet leadership created a fictitious world for its citizens to inhabit in maintaining that the Soviet state was constantly faced by a hostile and united capitalist camp, and used such a belief as a means of justifying strong internal controls over its own populace, and argued the necessity for an economic policy not too dissimilar to that typified by the old phrase "guns before butter"; the threat that capitalism was portrayed as representing was not a consequence of the structure of the totalitarian regime but rather a basic tenet of Marxist-Leninist ideology.

Finally, and to some extent following from the above criticism of this explanation of Soviet foreign policy, it is almost an open question as to whether or not totalitarianism gave rise specifically to a desire on the part of the Soviet leadership for world domination as a means of maintaining domestic control of their society. That possibility had to be considered that a foreign policy intended to ensure world domination would provoke aggression from the capitalist states, probably culminating in global warfare, which would endanger the maintenance of the Soviet leadership's "total" control of their own society.

e) **The Power Elite**. The basis of this explanation of Soviet foreign policy was the belief that the political elite within the Soviet Union had, as its prime concern, the maintenance and expansion of its own power base. In consequence policy, both domestic and foreign, was determined more or less exclusively by the effect which the elite calculated particular courses of policy will produce upon its hold of power. With this explanation, as Bell observed:

> "... emphasis is largely on personality and power groups, and less on the social systems and the way such systems can or cannot constrain these leaders."[25]

Rostow noted that the one persistent feature in the development of the Soviet state had been the importance which the political leadership had attached to the maintenance and aggrandisement of its own power irrespective of the cost to the mass of the Soviet population which this had necessitated.[26] Indeed, this elite objective had, according to Rostow, been given priority over other major Soviet objectives such as the expansion of Soviet power beyond the territorial confines of the USSR. The maintenance and extension of the power of the leadership was not simply a consequence of its desire to hold power, although this was undoubtedly an important consideration, but also had an ideological justification derived from the works of Lenin and more especially from the role he discerned for the party as the chief agency of progress. The linkage between the maintenance of power by the elite and the form that Soviet foreign policy takes, was revealed by Rostow's consideration of the nature of Soviet expansion which he attributed to the Marxist-Leninist goal of world communism, the fact that the internal stability of the USSR could only be maintained by portraying the non-Soviet world as one epitomised by hostility to Soviet existence and objectives; thus, in turn, justifying the hostile posture adopted by the Soviet state, and, finally, to the fact that as an international actor the Soviet Union could not operate successfully in pursuit of its objectives without a monopoly of internal power.

The views of Kennan were in similar vein, he maintains that the domestic and international situations confronting the Soviet regime at its foundation after the October Revolution of 1917, made it imperative for the party to establish dictatorial control, faced as it was with strong opposition from within and hostility from without; the latter leading eventually to direct intervention in the Soviet Union by the Entente. [27] Only once power had been consolidated in the Soviet state, Kennan contended would the leadership be in a position from which to advance to the attainment of the "good" for which the revolution had been waged. With the internal power consolidated the validity of this explanation Soviet foreign policy in the 1980s was questionable.

A final strand in the power elite theme was offered by the Kreminologists who:

"... focus primarily on the power struggle within the core elite and seek to identify ("who is doing in whom") within the Kremlin as a basis for predicting political events." [28]

This was essentially the internal operation of the kto-kovo couplet referred to earlier in the discussion of the cultural and personality explanation of Soviet foreign policy, with foreign policy being simply a reflection of the views of the victors in the internal struggle for power. The root causes of the internal power struggle were not always clearly discerned, but this was not altogether surprising given the difficulty of obtaining current and reliable information about domestic events in the Soviet Union; with the consequence that reliance had to be placed upon the subjective interpretation of such information as was available at any particular moment in time. Even when information was available its import was not always apparent:

"The shift in the top command of the Soviet Government, in particular the replacement of Mr Molotov with Mr Vishinsky as Foreign Minister, has unleashed such a flood of speculations and varying interpretations as to its meaning that it has thrown the world into new confusion and uncertainty."[29]

and,

"Premier Stalin, by shifting his key Ministers of Foreign Affairs and Foreign Trade ... has completely confused the governments of the Western world that await some clue as to the real import of this dramatic move,... The true import of the surprise Cabinet shift cannot be gauged."[30]

Conquest argued that the primary cause of internal power struggles was the differing interpretations given to Marxist-Leninist ideology by the senior officers of the

CPSU.[31] Thus it was argued that Soviet foreign policy could be broadly characterised as falling under one or other of two headings; encouraging the rapid development of Communism on a world scale, or, seeking gradual solutions to immediate problems; which group of policies was operative at a given time being a reflection of the ideological interpretations of the successful contestants in the internal power struggle. This view, however, did open up the possibility that the special merits and relevance of both of these broad foreign policy alternatives if of less importance than the gains to be made in the internal power struggle by their advocacy. Yet such an interpretation of Soviet foreign policy was not without its problems, for as Rosser discerned:

> "Undoubtedly, the internal struggle has dictated certain turns and twists in Soviet international strategy and tactics. But all Soviet leaders necessarily need to pay attention to the realities of international politics, to the external and internal factors determining Soviet capability. Otherwise, they cannot continue to rule. This in turn places a limit on the kinds of policies that a member of the elite can adopt at any one time, regardless of the demands of the power struggle." [32]

f) **Ideological**. The importance of the role of ideology in the formulation of Soviet foreign policy was to some extent, implicit in several of the explanations of that policy which have already been considered. Yet the role of ideology was also explicit in Soviet foreign policy, and whilst Marxist-Leninist ideology fell short of being a determinant, even less so the sole determinant, of that policy, it was possessed of a deep impact in as much as:

> "... (1) it establishes certain long range goals for Soviet foreign policy: (2) it provides the Soviet leaders with a system of knowledge on which to build their view of the world; (3) it gives them a method for analysing foreign policy problems; (4) it furnishes strategy and tactics to achieve the ultimate ends; (5) it ratifies the party's continuance in power, and thus the moral right of the party leaders even to make foreign policy; (6). it provides a unique method of control which has served to unify and co-ordinate the activities of communists all over the world; and (7) it serves as an important 'technique' for the expansion of Soviet influence."[33]

Yet any tendency to ascribe a deterministic function to ideology in the formulation of Soviet foreign policy, although a tempting one, was one which should be resisted; for, in the final analysis the Soviet Union was simply one among many actors on the international political stage and the scope for manoeuvre open to it was, in large measure, constrained and restricted by the roles that the other international actors themselves adopted. In short, the reality of international politics presents the Soviet leadership with situations which require from it responses which cannot be predicated purely on the basis of ideology; Realpolitik tempered ideological politics and whilst the "morality" of reality could be denied or contested the presence of reality could neither be discounted nor dismissed by reference to ideology.

Consideration of the "real world" of international politics called forth the final explanation of Soviet foreign policy to be discussed here, namely,

g) **National Interest**, under which may be subsumed concern with national security. Two difficulties immediately emerge; the problem of defining the national interest whilst accepting that all states have more than one, and the peculiar problem presented by the Soviet state whose leadership was formally committed to the advancement of an ideology which transcended Soviet national interest. This latter difficulty was, of course, one which publicly the Soviet leadership would not concede, as they were prepared to argue that any course of action advancing the interests of the USSR simultaneously advanced the interests of the international communist movement and vice versa; although this was open to question if attention was paid to splits in the socialist camp such as the Sino-Soviet hostility which developed in the late 1950s. Consideration of Soviet national interest, nevertheless, did imply that Soviet pronouncements should not be discounted simply as ideological prognostications nor merely as propaganda but rather should be treated as realistic assessments upon which Soviet foreign policy was founded and enacted. Whilst all states undoubtedly had a national interest, or more correctly national interests, it was no easy task to discern what those interests may be or what priority they may be given at a particular moment in time. What could, however, be realistically contended is that all states had a common, cardinal national interest the attainment of which was imperative; namely, national security or territorial integrity. Without the attainment of that basic and minimum requirement all other national interests were incapable of realisation, and in consequence, it must take precedence over all other state objectives, even when, as in the Soviet case, there existed a supposedly higher objective; the furthering of international communism. As Rosser noted,

> "When Soviet minimum security is in jeopardy, the Soviets present world communism in muted form. When the Soviets seem to feel relatively secure, the pursuit of world communism is more energetic. World Communism is the publicly stated, long-range maximum goal, always second in priority to the minimum goal of national security".[34]

Various writers have pointed to the importance of national security as a basis for assessing and explaining Soviet foreign policy. Rostow contends that, especially before 1939, Soviet foreign policy amounted to a series of responses to the international political climate of that period, and,

> "... took the form of such actions as were judged most likely, on a short-range basis, to maintain or expand the national power of the Soviet regime."[35]

Indeed, despite the changed international role of the USSR, occasioned by the Second World War, Rostow argued that,

> "... there is no evidence that the foreign policy criteria of the regime have changed."[36]

Likewise Black held that the immediate concerns of Soviet foreign policy had been determined primarily by the perceptions of Soviet security requirements; especially during the period 1921 to 1947.[37] Indeed, Churchill whilst conceding difficulty in comprehending Soviet foreign policy intentions did, nevertheless, adhere to the importance of Soviet perceptions of their national interest as providing the most fruitful guide:

"I cannot forecast to you the action of Russia. It is a riddle wrapped in a mystery inside an enigma; but perhaps there is a key. That key is Russian national interest"[38]

Those who argued for an explanation of Soviet foreign policy on an assessment of Soviet national interest were, in essence, maintaining that the Soviet leadership was constrained by the same considerations in determining its courses of action .as any other actor on the international scene. Sharp posed the question,

"If Soviet national interest is what the Soviet leaders take it to be, and if one argues - as one must - that their view of the world is derived from their adherence to Marxism-Leninism, isn't this another way of saying that Soviet behaviour is the result of ideological conditioning?" [39]

and answered that it was:

"Not quite. The point at issue is whether the 'pure' Soviet view of the world is an important guide to action, whether the ultimate aims of the Communist creed are operative in policy determinations." [40]

Sharp further believed that,

"... dwelling on the supposed impact of ideology on the leadership ... tends to ignore the degree to which

the pursuit of ultimate goals has been circumscribed in time and scope by considerations of the feasible."[41]

To illustrate this latter belief Sharp considered the relationship between Soviet national interests and its role as leader of the international communist movement, and cited five observations which suggested to him that,

"In the last analysis, virtually every instance where Moscow has claimed a victory for communism has depended on Soviet manipulation of traditional levers of national influence".[42]

The five observations which lead Sharp to this conclusion were:

"(1) early in its history the Communist International was transformed into a tool of Soviet foreign policy, at a time when no other tools were available to Moscow; (2) as soon as the Soviet state felt at all sure of its survival it reactivated the apparatus of foreign policy along more traditional lines; (3) under Stalin, the Third International was reduced to a minor auxiliary operation; (4) when the entire record of Soviet success and failure was summed up, the achievements were clearly attributable to Soviet power and diplomacy with no credit to the international Communist movement; (5) the Soviet appeal to foreign Communist parties was not dissimilar to the practice of various governments of different periods and persuasions to appeal for support abroad on the basis of some sort of affinity."[43]

From the range of explanations advanced two appear to provide a secure foundation from which to commence any analysis of Soviet foreign policy; namely, the ideological and national interest/security explanations; if for no other reason than that they were constants throughout the period following the Bolshevik seizure of power. Yet neither of these should be considered in isolation from the other, for ideology could be viewed as providing the framework within which Soviet national interests were perceived and pursued. Perhaps Hunt best depicted the relationship between the two and also the necessity to take both into account in explaining Soviet foreign policy,

> "There is no yardstick which permits a measure of the exact relationship between power politics and ideology in the policies which result; but surely neither factor can be ignored."[44]

and in doing so found common ground with Adams,

> "In sum Soviet foreign policy as conventional power politics is distinct from and at the same time inseparable from communist ideology... From this marriage of power politics and ideology stems the dualism that is the most obvious characteristic of Soviet foreign policy... And from this dualism arise many of the perplexing vacillations, the alternation of peace talks and threats of violence, the self-hindering practice of propagating revolution while simultaneously attempting to form alliances with bourgeois states."[45]

Although emphasis may most fruitfully be placed on explanations which took as their foci ideological and national security considerations, it is not beyond the limits of probability to conclude that, given the vacillations in Soviet foreign policy, different explanatory tools may have differing degrees of relevance and applicability at different times; since foreign policy is itself a response to perceptions of the domestic and international climates appertaining at a particular time and extrapolations from those perceptions. The mere existence of such a variety of explanations advanced at different times would, of itself, seem to imply that no one explanation is adequate to account for so complex a phenomenon as Soviet foreign policy.

References

1. See, for example, the account of the works of Herbert Simon and C E Lindblom in Sofer Cyril **Organizations in Theory and Practice**. Heinemann, London, 1972 pp157-163 and pp 166-167 and pp 171 -175.

2. Adams, Arthur E. **Readings in Soviet Foreign Policy: Theory and Practice**. D C Heath & Co Boston 1961 pp xiv-xv.

3   Triska Jan F and Finley David D. **Soviet Foreign Policy** Macmillan. New York 1969 pp xiv-xv.

4. Kerner Robert K. **The Urge to the Sea.** University of California Press, Berkeley, California 1942.

5. Cressey George B. **The Basis of Soviet Strength.** McGrow-Hill New York 1945 p 242.

6. Cressey George B. **How Strong is Russia?** Syracuse University Press, Syracuse NY 1954.

7. Strausz-Hupe Robert "The Western Frontiers of Russia" in Weigert Hans W et al (eds). **New Compass of the World** Macmillan. New York 1949.

8. Vernadsky George. **Political and Diplomatic History of Russia.** Little Brown. Boston 1936.

9. Bell Daniel. "Ten Theories in Search of Reality: The Prediction of Soviet Behaviour in the Social Sciences" in Dallin Alexander (ed) **Soviet Conduct in World Affairs** Greenwood Press Westport Corn 1975 pp 2-3.

10. Gorer Geoffrey and Rickman John. **The People of Great Russia.** Cresset Press London 1950.

11. Rosser Richard F. **An Introduction to Soviet Foreign Policy** Prentice Hall. Englewood Cliffs N J 1969 p 24.

12. Dicks H V. "Observations on Contemporary Russian Behaviour". **Human Relations.** Vol V No 2 May 1952. pp 111-175.

13. Bell op cit p 4.

14. Ibid.

15. Rosser op cit pp 24-25.

16. Leites Nathan C. **A Study of Bolshevism.** Free Press of Glencoe NY 1954. More recently Leites has undertaken a similar analysis of Khrushchev's

speeches and writings **Kremlin Moods**. The Rand Corp Santa Monica Calif 1964.

17. ibid p 527. For a useful precis of the main points of Leites' work see Bell's article in Dallin (ed) op cit pp 14-21.

18 Berdyaev Nikolai **The Origins of Russian Communism** G Bles London 1948.

19. Rosser op cit p 21.

20. ibid p 27.

21. Friedrich Carl J and Brzezinski Zbigniew K. **Totalitarian Dictatorship and Autocracy.** Harvard University Press. Cambridge Mass 1956 p 63.

22. ibid.

23. Arendt Hannah. **The Origins of Totalitarianism.** Allen and Unwin, London 1967.

24. Rosser op cit p 27.

25. Bell op cit p 12.

26. Rostow W W. **The Dynamics of Soviet Society.** W W Norton New York 1952.

27. Kennan George F. "**The Sources of Soviet Conduct**". Foreign Affairs, July 1947.

28. Bell op cit p 12.

29. Editorial New York Times 7 March 1949 quoted in Bishop Donald C. **Soviet Foreign Relations: Documents and Readings** Syracuse University Press. Syracuse NY 1952.

30. Dispatch by C L Sulzberger from Paris. New York Times 6 March 1949 quoted in Bishop ibid.

31. Conquest Robert. **Power and Policy in the USSR.** Macmillan New York 1961.

32. Rosser. op cit p 31.

33 ibid p 35.

34 ibid.

35. Rostow op cit p 136.

36. ibid.

37. Black Cyril. "The Pattern of Soviet Objectives" in Lederer Ivo J (ed) **Russian Foreign Policy.** Yale University Press. New Haven 1962 pp 3-38.

38 Churchill Winston S. Speech in London, 1 October 1939, also to be found in Churchill's The Gathering Storm.

39 Sharp Samuel L. "National Interest: Key to Soviet Politics" in Pentony Devere E (ed). **Soviet Behaviour in World Affairs: Communist Foreign Policies.** Chandler Publishing Co. San Francisco 1962. p 121.

40 ibid.

41 ibid.

42. ibid p 123.

43 ibid pp 122-123

43 Hunt Carew R N. "The Importance of Doctrine" in Pentony Devere E (ed) op cit p 115.

44 Adams op cit p xiii.

Chapter Two

Russo-German Relations from November 1914 to the Treaty of Brest-Litovsk March 1918

In August 1914 the German High Command launched an offensive on the Western Front based on a modified version of the Schlieffen plan devised in 1905.[1] It was thought that a sharp knockout blow could be dealt to France that would then allow the Central Powers to concentrate their resources against the might of Tsarist Russia in the East. However, as Martin Kitchen noted:

> *"Errors of planning and execution and the shortage of men and materials made it impossible for Schlieffen's plan to be realised and in spite of the extra-ordinary efforts of the German troops, it was the Germans who were in danger of being outflanked by the French."[2]*

> *"Germany had placed all her hopes on a swift victory in the West as the only way out of her precarious position. Now she was forced to fight a trench war and was locked in a battle of materials in which she was almost certain to be defeated."[3]*

As early as November 1914 the German Imperial Chancellor, Bethmann Hollweg, appreciated the serious implications raised by the failure of the Schlieffen plan and the prospect of being forced to conduct extensive military campaigns on two fronts. On November 19 1914 he wrote to the Under Secretary of State in the Foreign Ministry, Arthur Zimmermann:

"As long as Russia, France and England hold together it will be impossible for us to inflict such a defeat on out enemies as to achieve a satisfactory peace. We shall rather be running the risk of our own exhaustion. Either Russia or France must be prised off. If we succeed in bringing Russia to terms, which should be our primary objective, we could then deal France and England so crushing a blow that we could dictate peace terms even if the Japanese come across the sea to France and England, continuing to put fresh reinforcements on the field. But if Russia made peace, there is every reason to expect that France would also give in. Then if England made any trouble, we could bring it to heel by blockade..."[4]

The German Foreign Minister, Gottlieb von Jagow, was in general agreement with this analysis of the situation and during the following six months the German Foreign Ministry initiated several covert attempts to ascertain the attitude of the Tsar and his government to the possibility of a negotiated peace. To this end the services of the king of Denmark were sought as an acceptable intermediary between Berlin and St Petersburg,[5] while, on several occasions, the Grand Duke of Hesse, the brother of the Tsarina, urged his sister to persuade her husband to sanction a meeting between German and Russian representatives in Stockholm.[6] A former acquaintance of the Russian Royal Family, Maria Vasilchikova, was encouraged to write several personal letters to the Tsar indicating that she was in close contact with several high German Officials who emphasised their desire for peace with Russia, even to the extent of possibly agreeing to Russian control of the Dardonelles.[7] However, these attempts to use the extensive family links between the Russian and German monarchs to sound the political climate in St Petersburg appear to have been firmly rebuffed by Tsar Nicholas II. By his complete lack of response to the German initiatives the Tsar repeatedly underlined his intention to continue the war and, furthermore, to respect the declaration made by the Triple Entente on September 4 1914 rejecting the notion that any member of the Entente would be party to a separate peace.[8]

On another level an attempt to establish a channel of contact with the reportedly pro-German ex-premier of Russia, Count Witte through the mediation of the Swedish Foreign Minister, Wallenberg, was cut short by the death of Count Witte on March 12 1915.[9] With this apparent failure to establish contact with the ruling hierarchy in Russia the German Foreign Minister, in the summer of 1915, turned to an alternative line of approach. If the Russian government was not amenable to the conclusion of a separate peace it seemed that only a successful military campaign would force Russia out of the war or force the Tsar to reconsider his attitude towards a separate peace. Therefore, to this end, all possible steps should be taken to dislocate the Russian war effort. In pursuit of this goal the German Foreign Minister sought to create unrest and disturbance within

Russia by inciting rebellion against the many non-Russian peoples incorporated within the Russian Empire.[10] Initial hopes of promoting an uprising of the Moslem peoples of the Caucasus receded with the collapse of the Turkish campaign in that area in November 1914.[11] Despite this setback, a programme of financial and propaganda support for the various separatist groups in Georgia, Finland and the Ukraine was set into motion.

It was the limited success of this policy that brought to the fore the possibility of using not only nationalist groups within Russia to ferment dissent but also political factions that opposed the Tsarist regime. On September 30 1915, the German Minister in Bern, Romberg, reported that, through an Estonian agent, he had been informed that the Russian revolutionary, Lenin had outlined a programme based not only on the overthrow of the Tsar but also including:

"An offer of peace without any consideration for France, but on condition that Germany renounces all annexations and war-reparations."[12]

Romberg concluded:

"Even if, as I have said, the prospects of revolution are uncertain and Lenin's programme is therefore of doubtful value, its exploitation could still do invaluable service in enemy territory." [13]

The activities of Lenin and the Bolshevik party and also other revolutionary groups had been brought to the attention of the German Foreign Ministry by Alexander Helphand, also known as Parvus. Helphand had at one time been a respected member of the Russian revolutionary movement and still maintained extensive contacts with many of the leading figures in the movement.[14] With the outbreak of the war Helphand sought to manipulate the joint interest of the Germans and the Russian revolutionary groups in the downfall of the Tsar. On January 9 1915 he outlined his ideas to the German Ambassador in Constantinople:

"Germany would not be completely successful if it were not possible to kindle a major revolution in Russia. However there would still be a danger to Germany from Russia, even after the war, if the Russian Empire were not divided into a number of separate parts. The interests of the German Government were therefore identical with those of the Russian revolutionaries, who were already at work."[15]

The German Foreign Ministry was extremely receptive to a programme that promised not only to eliminate Russia from the war but also to considerably reduce Russian influence in Europe. It appeared that, through the promotion of national minorities within Russia and the many revolutionary groups, an opportunity was presented to weaken the core of the Russian state and to divide the Russian Empire into a series of small nations.

On the instructions of Gottlieb von Jagow, Helphand was invited to Berlin in January 1915. It was considered that Helphand held the perfect credentials to enable him to mobilise and co-ordinate dissent within Russia. In March 1915 Zimmermann approved the allocation of two million marks to finance revolutionary propaganda within Russia and requested the Ministry of the Interior to free Helphand of all travel restrictions within Germany and the neutral states.[17] With this backing Helphand established "the Institute for the Study of the Social consequences of the War" in Copenhagen. Manned largely by a staff of Russian emigres the object of the institute was to serve as a communications network and co-ordinating centre for the various revolutionary groups within Russia and those in exile throughout Europe.

Combined with the serious military setbacks suffered by the Russian army in the summer of 1915 Helphand's propaganda campaign seemed to be gathering momentum by the end of the year. On December 26 1915 von Jagow authorised the further allocation of one million roubles to finance preparations for the revolution that Helphand was confidently predicting for the following month.[18] However, Helphand had been over-optimistic in his calculations for although extensive street demonstrations and strikes marked the anniversary of Bloody Sunday on January 22 1916, the Tsarist Government was not deposed. Although it had been severely shaken the Russian government tottered blindly on, impervious to the counsel of both the British and French ambassadors to appease the Russian people by some form of political concession to the more moderate elements of the left and centre parties.[19]

In attempting to account for the failure of the abortive revolution Count Brockdorff-Rontzau, German Minister in Copenhagen, and a firm believer in the work Helphand was undertaking, pointed to the danger that a premature left wing rising could well have produced a counter-revolution by the extreme right wing elements supporting the continuation of the war.[20] It was therefore fortunate that the revolution had been stillborn for the revolutionary parties were obviously not yet fully prepared for a major uprising. Whatever the truth of the matter the failure of the Russian revolutionary parties to engineer the fall of the Tsar encouraged the Foreign Ministry to attempt once again to open contacts with the Russian government. Tentative links were established with Josef Kolyshenko, a former Under-Secretary of State in the Russian Finance Ministry and a member of the circle led by Prince Meshchersky that reportedly favoured a peace settlement with Germany.[21] However, progress was slow and limited and, more significantly, the balance of political forces within Germany itself was seen to be changing rapidly during the course of 1916.[22]

The appointment of Hindenburg as Chief of the General Staff and Ludendorff as First Quartermaster General in August 1916 was indicative of the growing power and influence of the military in the formulation of policy. Hindenburg and Ludendorff enjoyed enormously popular prestige as a result of their role in reversing the fortunes of the Russian Army on the Eastern Front. Now, as Martin Kitchen noted:

"The enormous popularity of Hindenburg, who had become a figure of almost mythical proportions, gave the supreme command a plebiscitary dimension which was to be exploited to the full by the military propagandists and chauvinist politicians. The country was to be united behind Hindenburg to achieve the "Hindenburg Victory" which would provide a panacea to all Germany's problems."[23]

Hindenburg and Ludendorff adhered rigidly to what they saw as the war aims of 1914, namely the annexation of Luxembourg and Longwy-Briery in the West and Courland and Lithuania in the East. Furthermore, German directed buffer states were to be set up in Belgium, Poland and the Ukraine under the umbrella of the House of Hohenzollern and a European Customs Union.[24]

Within Germany weight was given to the stance assumed by the military by the fact that only force of arms, rather than diplomacy, appeared to hold any prospect of ending the war.[25] However, the German Imperial Chancellor was under no illusion that such terms would be acceptable to the Entente nations. Furthermore, the impact of a war of attrition on the economies of Germany and Austria-Hungary suggested to Bethmann Hollweg that it could well be in Germany's interests to negotiate a settlement with the Entente. Hollweg was disturbed by the reports from Vienna. With the entry of Italy into the war the Austrian Chief of Staff, Conrad von Hotzendorff, had quickly realised that an early conclusion of the war was unlikely.[25] The implications of participation in a prolonged struggle were serious for Austria-Hungary for it threatened to produce only further dissension and division in an already infirm and weak Empire. However, attempts to induce Germany to moderate its war aims and look for a settlement with the Entente powers were continually thwarted by the reluctance of the German government to consider peace on anything other than their own terms.[27] As Gerhard Schulz comments:

"Given the military situation and the optimistic exuberance of the war mongering propagandists no German government would anyway then have dared to enter into peace negotiations on unfavourable or even uncertain terms."[28]

With the death of the Emperor Franz-Josef in November 1916 the new Emperor, Karl, immediately revealed his concern with the internal impact of the war on the Austro-Hungarian Empire.[29] The proposal made by the Entente, in their reply to President Wilson's peace initiative in January 1917, that after the war the Danubian Empire should be divided, only added to Karl's conviction that an immediate peace should be sought on the basis of the status quo ante bellum.[30] By passing German intransigence an attempt was made, through links with the royal house of Parma-Bourbon, to open links with Italy and France,[31] while on April 14 1917 the Emperor wrote to Kaiser Wilhelm II:

"It is perfectly clear that our military resources are coming to an end. In other words peace must be made at any price in the late summer or autumn."[32]

Caught between the conflicting demands of the Vienna government and the German Supreme Command the German Chancellor sought a compromise. In the Autumn of 1916, in an attempt to bring the war to an early conclusion, the German Supreme Command assured the Kaiser that the use of unrestricted submarine warfare in the Atlantic and the North Sea would enforce a blockade upon Britain that would result in a capitulation within six months.[33] Although Hollweg was forced to agree in principle to this scheme he worked actively to delay its initiation in the hope that the German Ambassador in Washington was correct in forecasting that President Wilson was preparing to launch a peace initiative.[34] However, when Wilson did not make foreign policy a major issue in his election campaign of November 1916, Hollweg appreciated that his last hope of a negotiated peace lay in adopting a suggestion made by the Austrian Foreign Minister, Burian, in October 1916 that the Central Powers should approach the Entente with a peace formula.[35]

Accordingly Hollweg wrote to Hindenburg on November 27 1916.

> *"On the whole I am entitled to assume that an offer of peace by us-the condition precedent for which, as I have said, is a favourable military situation on our side and for our enemies' prospects which contain no promise of victory - could in any case meet with resolute opposition from France alone."[36]*

Hindenburg agreed to the peace initiative on the understanding that military operations would continue and that if it failed the path would be cleared for the commencement of unrestricted submarine warfare. Sure in his conviction that Hollweg's plan would be rejected by the Entente powers Hindenburg observed with interest Hollweg's speech to the Reichstag on December 12 1916. Couched necessarily in vague terms in order to satisfy Hindenburg's stipulation that:

> *"...neither the Army nor the Homeland should suffer any injury."[37]*

Z.A.B. Zeman noted the implicit dilemma of Hollweg's position:

"The text of Bethmann's offer reflected the clash with the military behind the scenes: its language uneasily combined diplomatic restraint with the forthrightness of the German war lords."[38]

"At that point the weakness of Bethmann Hollweg's position lay revealed. He pursued peace not for its own sake alone, but also to keep the military at bay."[39]

"But he diminished the small chance of achieving it because he used the promise of peace to restrain the military and because he did not allow himself enough time for the execution of that policy."[40]

The absence of specific terms immediately engendered a suspicious and hostile reception from the Entente. In their official reply dated January 5 1917 the Entente powers concluded:

"It is with full realisation of the gravity but also of the necessities of the hour, that the Allied Governments, closely united and in perfect communion with their peoples, refuse to entertain a proposal without sincerity and without import."[41]

Unable to resist the pressure exerted by the Supreme Command and longer on January 9 1917 Hollweg conceded that:

"The U-Boat campaign is the "last card". A very serious decision! "But if the military authorities regard the U-Boat campaign as necessary I am not in a position to oppose them"."[42]

From this point onwards, any hope of a negotiated settlement receded rapidly. Inevitably, Hollweg's position had been severely limited by the stipulations established by the Supreme High Command, However, the final nail was put into the coffin by the declaration made by the Entente powers on January 12 1917 when their war aims were outlined as the reconstruction of Belgium, Serbia and Montenegro, the evacuation of occupied territories and the dissolution of the Ottaman and Austro-Hungarian Empires.[43] In reply, Hollweg could only note:

"That programme of war aims was not just a tactical maximum demand which could be reduced during negotiations. Nobody wanted to negotiate with us. Now already a dictated settlement was demanded."[44]

It therefore appeared that despite the frequent efforts of the German Foreign Ministry to engineer an understanding with the Entente Nations and in particular with Tsarist Russia, by January 1917 they were no nearer to their goal than when they set out in November 1914. On January 7 1917, in a Special Order of the Day, Tsar Nicholas II announced:

"To conclude a peace with Germany at the present would mean not to profit fully by the heroic efforts of the Russian Army and Fleet. These efforts... forbid us to even think of making peace before achieving a final and complete victory over the foe who dares to think, that, if he could begin the war, he can end it whenever he likes." [45]

Whatever his motives be they respect for the Allied agreements of September 1914 and April 1915, a desire to obtain the long sought-after control of the Dardonelles or simply just blind stubbornness, Nicholas revealed no inclination to sue for a separate peace with Germany. No doubt his determination was reinforced by the assertion of his military advisers that, although the army had suffered severe hardship, the troops would remain loyal. In January 1917 General Brussilov commanding the South Western Front recorded:

> ".. The discipline was still excellent at the moment, and had we taken the offensive there was no doubt that the troops would have done their duty as they had done in 1916."[46]

The prospect of a peace settlement had been at its zenith in 1916 when the Germanophile, Stürmer, was appointed Russian Premier. However, of this period the German Crown Prince records:

> "... I urged our leaders to grasp the opportunity. As a matter of fact in the course of the summer and in the early autumn numerous deliberations of a general character were carried on and terms considered; but all this took place privately among German diplomatists or extended only to conversations between them and the Higher Command. Practical deductions which might have resulted in the inauguration of relations with Stürmer were not discussed. We got no further than empty lamentations and futile complaints that the war had completely cut us off from all possibility of communicating with people across the frontier, that we could not join them, "the water was much too deep"." [47]

This conviction was seconded by General Ludendorff:

"There was never even a reasonable possibility of getting in touch with Stürmer nor the remotest suggestion of any move on his part. No-one really believed in the possibility of concluding peace with Russia."[48]

Indeed it is difficult to imagine on what terms a settlement could have been concluded between Germany and Russia given the collision of interests in Poland and the designs of the German Supreme Command in the Baltic states. Furthermore, Russian ambitions in relation to Constantinople and the Balkan nations could only have been satisfied at the expense of Germany's allies, the Habsburg and Ottaman Empires. While both powers adhered to their respective war aims of 1914, nourished on a belief in an eventual victory of arms, there appeared little ground for compromise. This position was tacitly admitted in November 1916 when the intention was announced to sponsor an independent Polish state linked to the House of Hohenzollern and with a German trained army. [49]This blatant attempt to place Poland within the German sphere of influence only served to further underline the German conviction that a negotiated settlement with the Tsarist regime was impossible and, as Zeman noted, other methods would have to be employed:

"The Russians were to be harried by subversive activities; military defeat would facilitate anti-war propaganda; the government bent on pursuit of war would be overthrown, and peace would be concluded

*with the revolutionaries. In this reckoning there was
no longer a place for the Tsarist government."[50]*

However the Tsarist government was increasingly
blind to the impact being made on the Russian nation
by suicidal war losses and extreme shortages of
virtually all the basic living commodities. The country
was seen to be ruled by a rapidly changing succession
of ministries, all of which carried the common stamp of
corruption and inefficiency. Only personal loyalty to the
Tsar and the crumbling "Union Sacré" held the nation
together and these institutions drew heavily on a well of
goodwill and obedience that was rapidly running dry.
As Wheeler-Bennett commented:

*"Revolution was being planned from both above and
from below, and the watchword of both revolutionary
parties was Peace - Peace to save autocracy, or Peace
to hasten the "dictatorship of the Proletariat".[51]*

*"At the beginning of February 1917 'The Union of
the Russian People' advised the Tsar to "restore order
in the state at **whatever cost**, and be certain over
the victory of the foe **within**, who long since had
become more dangerous and more relentless than the
foreign enemy".[52]*

Between the extremists of the left and right stood
the liberal factions of the Duma who urged immediate
reform in a desperate attempt to save the situation:

*"Their pleas were shattered against the lifeless
detachment of the Emperor, and, in face of
impending disaster, they returned to the political
salons of Petrograd...[53]*

"Enwrapped in his impenetrable mantle of apathy Nicholas II foiled every attempt to save him from himself."[54]

It is surprising, therefore, that the abdication of the Tsar on March 15 1917, following the escalation of the bread riots and the abortive attempt to dissolve the Duma, was an event that had not been expected or predicted by any of the varied political factions in the Russian capital. Neither the extreme left or right wing groups had the influence or the organisation to assume power:

"The only people who were prepared to pick it up were those liberal constitutionalists who favoured the prosecution of the war for democracy and freedom, regardless of the fact that the vast majority of the Russians yearned for peace and had, in fact, made the Revolution in its name."[55]

"Of sheer political impotence and well-measuring ineptitude history has few more striking examples than that of the Provisional Government which took office on the abdication of the Tsar."[56]

"It was lacking both in all means of enforcing its authority and in those supports of tradition which had so long buoyed up the monarchy, and it failed signally to create any new supports of its own. It was not so much revolutionary as idealistic and proved utterly incapable of interpreting or controlling the vast forces of unrest which had brought it to power."[57]

Within the Provisional Government the portfolio for foreign affairs was assigned to Paul Milyukov, a founder of the Kadet Party in 1905 dedicated to constitutional reform within Russia. Milyukov's conviction that the internal upheaval of March 1917 need not affect Russia's external policy was indicated in his first pronouncement on policy on March 18 1917. Russia, he declared:

"... will remain mindful of the international engagements entered into by the fallen regime.... and will fight by their (Allies) side against the common enemy to the end."[58]

This appeared to be endorsed by the Declaration of the Provisional Government on March 20 1917:

"The Government will sacredly observe the alliances which bind us to other powers, and will unswervingly carry out the agreements entered into by the Allies."[59]

Undoubtedly Milyukov's resolve to honour the Tsarist pledges to the Entente powers was influenced by the belief that Russia could still reap the rewards outlined in the secret treaties of 1914 and 1915.

However, although the Provisional Government retained nominal control of the country, it was increasingly apparent that the political vacuum created by the disintegration of the Tsarist administrative machinery had been largely filled by the creation of a network of Workers', Soldiers' and Peasants' Soviets that had been established in many areas of the country. It was the Soviets that held the real power throughout the country and were receptive to the desires and aspirations of the Russian people in their hunger for "Peace, bread and land".[60]

Dominated largely by the parties of the left an immediate gulf was apparent in the field of foreign policy when on March 27 1917 the Petrograd Soviet issued a Proclamation to the Peoples of the World urging them:

> "...to take into their own hands the question of war and peace ... to refuse to serve as an instrument of conquest and violence in the hands of kings, landowners and bankers...."[61]

This assault on the traditional concepts of diplomacy was continued through the left wing press:

> "Secret diplomacy is the natural offspring of autocracy, it is afraid of light and prefers to hatch its duty plots in darkness.... You cannot pour new wine into old bottles. The power, created by the revolution, must also make a decisive break with the traditions of men like Izvolski and Stuemer in the realm of foreign policy."[62]

Under severe attack from the Petrograd Soviet on April 27 1917 the Provisional Government was forced to qualify its stance.

> "...the purpose of free Russia is not domination over other nations or seizure of their national possessions, or forcible occupation of foreign territories, but the establishment of stable peace on the basis of self determination of peoples."[63]

However Milyukov refused to renounce his ambition to expand Russian influence in Poland and the

Black Sea and when transmitting the Provisional government's statement to the Diplomatic corps in Petrograd he added a covering note stating that:

> *"the Provisional Government while safe-guarding the rights of our own country will, in every way, observe the obligations assumed towards our Allies."*[64]

This apparent reaffirmation of the annexationist treaties concluded by the Entente during the war infuriated the Soviet to the extent that, in order to avoid a further uprising, the Premier of the Provisional Government, Prince Lvov, was forced to drop Milyukov from the government and incorporate several eminent socialists in a new cabinet. On May 18 1917 the government announced that it:

> *"..spurns the idea of a separate peace and proclaims openly that it is its aim to bring about, at the earliest possible date, a general peace, without either imposing its domination over any nation, or taking away any nations possessions, or forcibly annexing foreign territory."*.[65]

This represented a significant victory for the power of the Petrograd Soviet but failed to resolve the inherent contradictions in the policy of the Soviet. As the appeal made by the Petrograd Soviet on May 15 1917 revealed, the Soviet recognised the peoples' desire for peace and called for a:

> *"...peace without annexation and indemnities on the basis of self-determination of peoples....*

It furnishes the platform on which the toiling masses of all countries -belligerent and neutral - could and should come to an understanding in order to establish a lasting peace."[66]

However it was emphasised that: The Russian Revolutionary Democracy does not want a separate peace which could free the hands of the Austro-German Alliance.[67]

As Trotsky noted:

"The agitators had been telling the masses of soldiers that the Tsarist Government had been driving them to slaughter for no object or sense; but those who replaced the Tsar were able neither to change the character of the war in any way not to make a fight for peace."[68]

Z.A.B. Zeman concluded:

"In this way, the revolutionary foreign policy of the Soviet majority involved itself in fatal contradiction. It was committed to the defence of Russia while it waited for a socialist peace: it had to encourage the soldiers to fight while agitating for peace."[69]

Furthermore at a time when the Petrograd Soviet was calling on the Russian war machine to contrive the struggle it issued the infamous Prikoz No 1 which suppressed all marks of respect within the army when off duty and called for the establishment of Soldiers' Councils in each unit to be consulted on all questions of discipline and administration. General Brussilov, who had been appointed Supreme Commander-in-chief of the Russian Army in May 1917 noted:

"In May the troops on all the fronts began definitely to refuse to obey orders, and no steps could be taken to stop them.

What was even worse was that, although the Mensheviks and Social Revolutionaries thought it necessary to maintain the Army in being and did not wish to break with the Allies, they themselves brought about its destruction by issuing the accursed Prikoz No 1 and the Declaration of Soldiers' Rights, which utterly undermined the discipline without which no army can exist."[70]

In Germany the Supreme High Command watched events in Russia with evident relish. Of the March revolution Hindenburg observed:

"Hitherto the unwieldy Russian Colossus had hung over the whole European and Asiatic world like a nightmare."[71]

"Now that it had materialised it aroused in me no feeling of political satisfaction but rather a sense of military relief."[72]

General Ludendorff confirmed this opinion:

"How often had I not hoped for a revolution in Russia in order that our military burden might be alleviated."[73]

Although the Provisional Government had elected to continue the war a virtual unofficial armistice descended on the Eastern Front in the immediate months following the revolution. Ludendorff expressly ordered the Chief of the General Staff on the Eastern

Front, General Max Hoffmann, to refrain from mounting any further offensives so that troops could be transferred to the Western Front while at the same time the new Russian government was subject to peace feelers from Berlin. As Ludendorff commented in his memoirs:

> "I was unwilling to do anything which, even in appearance, might injure a real prospect of peace."
> 73A

However, Hoffmann considered that the Russian army, although severely shaken, was still an effective fighting force and therefore, as he noted in his diary on April 30 1917, he had no intention of launching an offensive:

> "In any case, the Russian Revolution is a godsend to us, for if there had been heavy fighting in the East at the same time we should have been up against it."[74]

The efforts of the German Foreign Ministry to fuel revolution within Russia appeared to have been well rewarded. It is calculated that between August 1914 and January 1918 the Germans spent twenty six million Marks to finance various forms of subversion within Russia.[75] However, the advent of the March revolution and the refusal of the Provisional Government to seek a peace agreement with the Central Powers caused the German Foreign Ministry to re-assess its strategy. After the proclamation of an independent Polish state in November 1916 the German Foreign Ministry had tacitly abandoned its dual policy of attempting to seek an agreement with the Tsar while simultaneously trying to undermine the Russian war effort by financing propaganda and contacts with the various elements opposed to the Tsar within Russia. In turning almost exclusively to the support of factions looking to end the war and depose the Tsar, German finance had embraced such diverse groups as the extreme nationalist and revolutionary parties at one end of the spectrum to right wing elements in government and business circles who sought to end the war to prevent revolution at the other extremity. However, now that the Tsar had abdicated and the Provisional Government had not sought peace terms, the German Foreign Ministry was forced to a further re-assessment of its policy. Increasingly the intention of the Foreign Ministry was drawn to the activities of the extreme left wing revolutionary groups who not only opposed the continuation of the war but also through their agitation and propaganda accelerated the disintegration of the Russian army and the morale of the domestic population.[76]

As early as March 23 1917 Zimmermann, the new State Secretary to the Foreign Ministry had concluded:

"Since it is in our interests the influence of the radical wing of the Russian revolutionaries should prevail, it would seem to me advisable to allow transit to the revolutionaries there."[77]

Therefore when, in the first week of March, a representative of the various Russian emigres in Switzerland approached Romberg, the German Minister in Bern, with an enquiry concerning the possible repatriation of emigres to Russia, the German Foreign Ministry was able to give its immediate approval to the principle of assisting Russian repatriation.

The outbreak of the March revolution had occurred while Lenin was in exile in Zurich. He immediately interpreted the activity in Russia as the initial move in the long awaited Socialist revolution. As early as November 1 1914 Lenin had predicted in an address to the Central Committee of the Bolshevik Party:

"The greater the sacrifices imposed by the war the clearer it will become to the mass of the workers that the opportunists have betrayed the workers' cause and that the weapons must be turned against the government and the bourgeoisie of each country."

At the Zimmerwald Conference of September 1915 and the Kienthal Conference of April 1916 Lenin restated his conviction that the European socialist movement should oppose the war and that a truly democratic peace could only be achieved if the war was transformed into a class based civil war with the masses rising to overthrow the bourgeoisie. As reports reached Zurich of the events in Russia in March and April of 1917 Lenin appreciated that if his vision was to be realised he must return to Russia at the earliest possible moment. The Bolshevik leadership in Petrograd appeared confused and prepared to adopt a conciliatory attitude to the Provisional government. In his "Letters from Afar" to the Bolshevik party newspaper "Pravda" Lenin severely rebuked his colleagues for supporting rather than undermining the government's attempts to continue the war.[80]Meanwhile Lenin's proposal that he should travel heavily disguised through France and Holland to Sweden en route to Russia was rejected by his colleagues as completely impracticable.[81]

Lenin was aware that the Menshevik faction in Switzerland were attempting to negotiate with the German Minister for passage through Germany to Sweden. This option had at first seemed distasteful to Lenin for he feared being branded as a German agent. However, on April 3 1917, he asked Fritz Platten, Secretary of the Swiss Social Democratic Party to mediate between himself and the Germans concerning his immediate return to Russia. Romberg, when reporting his conversation with Platten to the German Foreign Ministry, commented:

> *"Since their immediate departure would he greatly*
> *in our interests, I urgently recommend that*
> *permission should be granted at once, accepting the*
> *conditions laid down."[82]*

On April 5 and April 6 1917 Romberg reported that approximately twenty members of Lenin's party were ready to leave Switzerland on the understanding that they would not have any contact with the outside world while travelling by train through Germany except through Platten as an intermediary.[83] The following day Bussche, Under Secretary of State in the Foreign Ministry, replied that the conditions were acceptable except for the role of Platten as intermediary.[84]The party left Switzerland on April 9 and arrived at Malmo on April 12 en route to a triumphant reception at the Finland Station in Petrograd on April 16 1917.

The role played by the German Foreign Ministry and Military High Command in facilitating the return of Lenin and his followers to Russia has been the subject of much controversy in terms of to what extent the Bolshevik movement was promoted by the Germans to serve German ambitions. Certainly Lenin went to extreme lengths to deny that the Bolshevik movement was in any way an agent for the forces of the Central Powers. On April 12 1917 Lenin wrote to an associate in Stockholm, Ganetsky:

"The bourgeoisie (Plekhanov) are attacking us frantically for having passed through Germany. They are trying to stir up the soldiers against us. So far they have not succeeded: we have supporters and loyal ones ."[85]

In August 1917 following the storm surrounding the Malinovsky affair and further accusations that the Bolshevik party had extensive links with the Germans, Lenin replied:

"The base slander, raised by the bourgeoisie, that Ganetsky and Kollantay, and many others, were spying, or aiding it, is, of course, a low means of hiding the attack on the Internationalists on the part of our brave "Republicans" who wish to differentiate themselves profitably from Czarism by slander."[86]

"A pamphlet out to be brought out at once against this monstrous Dreyfusism and slander, and without sparing labour, trouble or money, so as to brand the slanderers and to help those who have been arrested on account of the slander."[87]

However, despite these declarations, there is little doubt that the German Foreign Ministry aided and supported the Bolshevik cause both directly and indirectly during this period in the quest to undermine the war effort and, if possible, to establish a regime in

Russia amenable to the conclusion of peace. David Shub presents evidence that indicates that through the mediation of Ganetsky, Lenin was in frequent contact with the German agent Helphand to organise what he concluded could only be a flow of financial assistance from Germany for the Bolshevik party. Shub claims that extensive amounts of cash were turned over by Helphand to Ganetsky, who was at that time a member of the Foreign Bureau of the Bolshevik Central Committee. Ganetsky later claimed that these funds were then transmitted through the Russian Embassy in Stockholm direct to Petrograd. However, further evidence would seem to indicate that a more circuitous route was used, involving an account held by a Madame Sumenson in the Siberian Bank in Petrograd through which funds were channelled to Kozlovsky, a Bolshevik member of the Soviet Executive Committee.[88] Not surprisingly both Lenin and Trotsky vehemently denied that they received any money from Ganetsky and Kozlovsky or that the Bolshevik party had any dealings with a Madame Sumenson. However, in a letter to Ganetsky dated June 12 1917, Lenin wrote:

"Until today we have received nothing, literally nothing from you, neither letters nor packets nor money."[89]

Several days later in a further letter Lenin noted:

"The money (2,000) from Kozlovsky received."[90]

Although it is difficult to substantiate the claim made by Edward Bernstein, the German Social Democratic leader, that the Bolsheviks received up to fifty million gold marks from the Germans, it would appear that Lenin and his followers did receive extensive financial assistance from the German Foreign Ministry from the period March 1917 onwards.[9] In September 1917 the State Secretary to the Foreign Ministry, Kuhlmann, stated:

> *"The military operations on the Eastern Front, which were prepared on a large scale and have been carried out with great success, were seconded by intensive undermining activities inside Russia on the part of the Foreign Ministry".*[92]

As Kuhlmann noted, in these calculations the Bolshevik Party played a prominent role:

> *"The Bolshevik movement could never have attained the scale or the influence which it has today without our continual support"*

Undoubtedly the German Foreign Ministry actively endorsed the Bolshevik party programme based upon opposition to the authority of the Provisional Government and agitation for a Russian withdrawal from the war. On April 21 1917 a report to the Foreign Ministry based on information from an agent in Stockholm concluded:

> *"Lenin's entry into Russia successful. He is working exactly as we would wish."*[94]

Furthermore, the Foreign Ministry went to great lengths to camouflage its links with the Bolsheviks in order not to impair Lenin's credibility with the Russian people. On August 18 1917 Bussche, Under Secretary of State in the Foreign Ministry, wrote to Brockdorff-Rantzau, the Minister in Copenhagen:

"The suspicion that Lenin is a German agent has been energetically countered in Switzerland and Sweden at our instigation."[95]

In a sense this statement contained a grain of truth. Lenin accepted German aid because the Bolshevik party desperately needed financial support and because, in that short term, both parties had a common goal in their dislike of the Provisional Government and their quest for peace. Therefore Lenin served German interest only in so far as they coincided with his own strategy.[96] In the short term this was perfectly acceptable to the Germans. As Ludendorff later noted:

"By sending Lenin to Russia our Government had moreover assumed a great responsibility. From the military point of view his journey was justified for Russia had to be laid low."

However, Hindenburg and Ludendorff subsequently claimed that they did not appreciate the possible long term implications of this policy.

Lenin brought a cohesion and sense of purpose to the Bolshevik party that had been absent previously. Although his call for the seizure of power by the Soviets and an end to the war suffered two severe setbacks with the victory of the Menshevik proposals at the All-Russian Congress of Soviets in June 1917 and the failure of the Bolshevik putsch in July 1917,[98] the failure of the Provisional Government to capitalise on these opportunities allowed the Bolsheviks to continue their agitation against the government. Kerenski, the new head of the Provisional Government, still clung to the illusion that the Russian war machine could fight on while the basis for a collective peace treaty, in concert with the Entente powers, was sought. However, his hopes were dealt a serious blow with the collapse of the Russian offensive in July 1917.[99] Indeed the initial Russian advance soon became a full scale retreat. General Brussilov, the Russian Supreme Commander-in-Chief, noted:

> *"At the front the position was lamentable. All discipline had disappeared, and its very foundations were shattered. The Army was falling to pieces."*[100]

The German Commander, General Max Hoffmann, felt that the German Armies could have quite easily captured Petrograd if the advance had not been brought to a premature halt by the need to transfer troops to the Western Front and a further initiative by the Foreign Ministry to the Kerenski government for a peace settlement.[101]

Discontent with the Kerenski regime was manifest not only from the ranks of the revolutionary left wing parties but also from the forces of conservatism. In September 1917 General Kornilov with a force of Cossack and Caucasian troops attempted to depose the government only to be blocked when the railway workers refused to provide transport for Kornilov's divisions to Petrograd.[102] In essence the Kornilov putsch sounded the death knell for the Provisional Government. Not only did it sever Kerenski's tenuous links with the army leadership but also convinced the lower ranks of the army and the working classes that their only salvation from a further right wing coup lay in supporting Lenin's advocation of a class revolution with a transfer of power to the Soviets and an end to the war.[103]

In October the Moscow and Petrograd Soviets fell under the domination of the Bolshevik party. While the Provisional Government, isolated and increasingly impotent, cast about for a decisive lead in its policy the Bolsheviks established themselves in the Smolny Institute from where they planned and directed the uprising of November 7 1917. As Wheeler-Bennett noted:

> "The Kerensky regime perished, as it had lived, ingloriously and with infirmity of purpose. Red guards had been organised on a large scale in expectation of fierce opposition, but the Provisional Government simply melted away."[104]

The Provisional Government fell essentially because it failed to admit that given the war weariness of Russia it was a fatal contradiction to call for peace while urging the army to fight on while a settlement was sought. Only the Bolsheviks promised to satisfy immediately the call for "Peace, Bread and Land". However, in attempting to assess the role played by the German Foreign Ministry in the revolution Zeman commented:

> "Lenin and the Bolsheviks recognised no treaties or obligations, nor, until November 1917, were they limited by any ties of political power. Their rise was watched with satisfaction in Berlin since the German leaders expected Lenin and the Bolsheviks to help them to achieve the elusive objective of a separate peace. But between Lenin and the Germans there were no bonds either of sympathy or of contract.[105] Lenin appreciated that one of his first steps had to be the launching of an initiative to bring the war with the Central Powers to an early conclusion."

Accordingly on November 8 1917 the Bolshevik government issued the Decree on Peace:

"The workers' and peasants' government created by the revolution of October 24-25 and relying on the Soviets of Workers', Soldiers' and Peasants' Deputies call upon all the belligerent peoples and their governments to start immediate negotiations for a just, democratic peace."[106]

"...by such a peace the government means an immediate peace without annexation (ie without the seizure of foreign lands without the forcible incorporation of foreign nations) and without indemnities."[107]

After calling for the abolition of all forms of secret diplomacy, the publication of all secret treaties and agreement on an immediate armistice for three months, the decree ended with a plea to the European proletariat to:

"...understand the duty that now faces them of saving mankind from the horrors of war and its consequences ..., by comprehensive determined and supremely vigorous action will help us to bring to a successful conclusion the cause of the emancipation of the toiling and exploited masses of the population from all forms of slavery and from all forms of exploitation."[108]

The declaration was indicative of the basic concepts incorporated in Lenin's view of the international situation of that time. In September 1917 in his pamphlet entitled "Tasks of the Revolution", Lenin had maintained that an offer of peace based on rejection of annexations or indemnities:

> *"will be greeted by all the nations with such tremendous sympathy, there will arise such a great epoch making outburst of enthusiasm and such universal indignation against the prolongation of this predatory war, that we shall most probably at once obtain an armistice and consent to the opening of peace negotiations"[109]*

> *"In the least probable event, viz, if not a single belligerent country consents even to an armistice, then the war will really become an enforced war, a really just and defensive war."[110]*

Lenin seemed convinced that the example set by the Russian Revolution, coupled with an emotive appeal to the European proletariat, would result in spontaneous uprisings throughout Europe that would force the belligerent governments to enter into negotiations or be swept away by a tide of revolutionary zeal. This would precipitate a peace engineered by social revolution as the proletariat realised the need to free itself from the interests of the bourgeoisie.

However, the ambassadors in Petrograd representing France, Britain and the United States not only agreed to ignore the Decree on Peace but also to regard the Military High Command based at Moghilev, as the governing body within Russia. In their desire to prevent Russia from concluding a peace settlement with the Central Powers, the Allied ambassadors repeatedly urged General Dukhonin to respect the secret treaties of

1914 and 1915 and continue the war. This policy appeared to be paying a dividend when, on November 21 1917, Dukonin ignored an order from the Commissar of War in Petrograd to open negotiations for an armistice with the German forces. However, the November revolution had left the officer corps torn between their desire to fulfil their commitments to the Entente and continue the war and the realisation that the army was rapidly disintegrating and that the men no longer held any faith or respect for their officers. The Bolsheviks were able to exploit the declining influence of the officer corps and when the Commissar for War, Krylenko, arrived at Moghilev on December 2 1917, the garrison was quickly persuaded that Dukhonin was a traitor to the revolution and that Krylenko should be recognised as the new Commander-in-Chief of the army.[112]

Despite this initial victory in winning over the support of large elements of the armed forces to their cause, the Bolshevik hierarchy in Petrograd was increasingly concerned by the lack of response to the Decree on Peace from not only the Allied governments but also the European proletariat. Lenin appreciated that popular support for the Bolshevik government could only be maintained if the government was seen to be taking immediate steps to end the war. Therefore, while not discarding his ultimate faith in the imminence of a European Revolution, Lenin instructed Trotsky, as Commissar for Foreign Affairs, to approach the German Supreme Command with a proposal for an armistice.[113] In reply to accusations that this represented a quest for a separate peace that infringed the Entente agreements,

Trotsky informed the Allied Military Missions in Petrograd:

> *"As long as Allied Governments answer with bare 'no recognition' of us and our initiative we will follow our own course appealing to the peoples after the governments. Should the results of the appeal bring separate peace, which we do not want, responsibility will fall completely upon the Allied Governments."*[114]

In essence, though, the Bolshevik government was not concerned with the implications of a separate peace or the abrogation of previous agreements. It was widely believed that the armistice would merely serve as a breathing space before the inevitable rising of the European proletariat. As Trotsky observed:

> *"Our future dealings will be with the German peasants and workers clad in soldiers' coats. There, in their midst, grows our future popular soldiers diplomacy."*[115]

The Bolshevik request for an armistice was favourably received in Berlin. Certainly the Germans had few illusions about the nature of the Bolshevik government. On November 12 1917 the Counsellor of the Stockholm Legation had reported to the Imperial Chancellor, von Hertling:

> *"In contrast to the Mensheviks, the Bolshevik theorists had jettisoned the parliamentary theory as early as 1906, setting up the idea of the revolutionary dictatorship of a small committee of determined leaders as their only possible course."*[116]

"Even if the power of the Bolsheviks in Russia only lasts a few weeks, the country will almost certainly have to face terror such as even France under Marat hardly experienced."[117]

The resignation of Bethmann Hollweg in July 1917 had been indicative of the increasingly central role played by the Supreme High Command in German politics from 1916 onwards.[118]

As Gerhard Schulz noted:

"...to an increasing extent the Army leadership adapted itself to the demands of total warfare by creating new spheres of regimentation in political and social life. Towards the end of the war the supreme commanders wielded more power than any military authority in the history of Russia or of Germany."[119]

Brushing aside suggestions that Germany should moderate its war arms in order to seek a peace of conciliation with the Entente nations, Hindenburg and Ludendorff pressed vigorously for the launching of a massive offensive in the West that would bring the war to a successful conclusion before the full potential of the United States Armed Forces could be realised in Europe. However, the neutralisation of the Russian army in the East, to allow movement of troops to the Western Front, was an important pre-requisite for this policy. Although the revolutions of March and November 1917 had drastically dislocated the fighting potential of the Russian army Ludendorff concluded that a campaign to conquer the vast territories of the Russian Empire would deny the Western Front desperately needed resources of manpower and materials. Therefore, the

Bolshevik offer of an armistice came as a lifeline to Ludendorff. As Hoffmann recorded in his memoirs:

"General Ludendorff telephoned to me and asked: "Is it possible to negotiate with these people?" I answered: "Yes, it is possible to negotiate with them. Your Excellency needs troops and this is the best way to get them"."[120]

For once the Austro-Hungarian government was in full agreement with the German Supreme Command in accepting the Bolshevik offer of an armistice. With the publication of the secret treaties between the Entente nations by the Bolshevik government, it was revealed that the Entente was aiming for the virtual dismemberment of the Austro-Hungarian Empire. Although enthusiasm for the war in Vienna and Budapest was rapidly waning, given the distaste of the German Supreme Command for conciliation, it appeared that only a military victory in concert with Germany could save the Habsburg Empire.[121]

With the need for an armistice on the Eastern Front, the survival of the Bolshevik government had become an important priority for the German government. On November 9 1917 Kuhlmann recommended that fifteen million marks be allocated to promote political propaganda in Russia,[122] while on November 23 1917 the Under Secretary of State, Bussche, urged that the Petrograd government be provided with further financial assistance to assist it in overcoming its difficulties.[123] Furthermore, the German press was instructed to avoid making friendly gestures towards the Bolshevik government that might compromise the regime in the eyes of the Russian people. The attitude of the German Foreign Ministry to the situation was summarised by Kuhlmann on December 3 1917:

"The disruption of the Entente and the subsequent creation of political combinations agreeable to us constitute the most important war aim of our diplomacy. Russia appeared to be the weakest link in the enemy chain. The task therefore was gradually to loosen it, and, when possible, to remove it. This was the purpose of the subversive activity we caused to be carried out in Russia behind the front - in the first place promotion of separatist tendencies and support of the Bolsheviks. It was not until the Bolsheviks had received from us a steady flow of funds through various channels and under different labels that they were in a position to be able to build up their main organ, **Pravda**, *to conduct energetic propaganda and appreciably to extend the original narrow basis of their party. The Bolsheviks have now come to power; how long they retain power cannot be yet foreseen. They need peace in order to strengthen their own position; on the other hand it is entirely in our interest that we should exploit the period while they are in power, which may be a short one, in order to attain firstly an armistice and then, if possible, peace. The conclusion of a separate peace would mean the achievement of the desired war aim, namely a breach between Russia and her Allies."*[124]

However, in this document, which was later endorsed by the Kaiser,[125] Kuhlmann attempted to look beyond the immediate problem of obtaining an armistice. He considered that if a breach could be forced between Russia and the Allies, the Russian government would then be forced to look towards Germany for financial aid. This might allow Germany to take effective control of Russia's vast reserves of raw materials. Although Kuhlmann appreciated that Austro-Hungary also held ambitions in respect of possible domination of Poland he was confident that Germany was in a strong enough position to enforce its viewpoint.

It was therefore with great satisfaction that the German High Command received, on November 27 1917, a request from the Russian Supreme Commander in Chief for a military armistice. It was agreed that conversations should be opened on December 2 1917 at Brest-Litovsk, the German military headquarters for the Eastern Front. In an effort to induce the Entente nations to participate in the proposed discussions on November 28 1917 Trotsky made a broadcast to "The Peoples of the Belligerent Countries":

"We offered to conclude a new open agreement based on the principles of consent and co-operation. The reply of the official and semi-official representatives of the ruling classes in the Allied countries was a refusal to recognise the Soviet Government and enter into an agreement with it for peace negotiations. The Government of the victorious revolution does not require recognition from the professional representatives of capitalist diplomacy, but we do ask the people: "Does reactionary diplomacy express their ideas and aspirations? Are they willing to allow the diplomats to let the great opportunity for peace offered by the Russian revolution slip through their fingers?" The answer to these questions must be

*given without delay, and it must be an answer in
deeds and not merely in words."*[126]

Despite the absence of a positive response from
either the governments or peoples of the Entente
powers, on December 2 1917, the Russian Armistice
delegation crossed the German lines at Dünaburg en
route to Brest-Litovsk. The delegation had been hastily
assembled and was led by Adolf Abramovich Joffe, a
Bolshevik who had recently been released from
imprisonment in Siberia and with a reputation as an
intellectual within the party.

The Bolsheviks were also represented by Leo
Kamenev, Trotsky's brother-in-law and Sokolinov who
was later destined to become Soviet Ambassador to
London. To conform with the Bolshevik Party's tacit
alliance with the Social Revolutionaries, Anastasia
Bitsenko was included in the delegation. Finally the
delegation was completed by the inclusion of a soldier,
sailor, worker and a peasant. As Wheeler-Bennett
commented:

> *"They were produced for 'window dressing' and had
> no other duties than to create an atmosphere of
> revolutionary democracy..."*[127]

Attached as advisers to the delegation were nine
military and naval officers led by Admiral Altvater:

> *"These unfortunates, placed by fate in a false and
> humiliating position, were in a purely advisory
> capacity and had no voice or power of voting."*[128]

The German Foreign Ministry was represented by
the presence of Baron von Rosenberg. However, the
German delegation was led by Major-General Max

Hoffmann, Chief of Staff on the Eastern Front. Of Hoffmann,Wheeler-Bennett noted:

> "...*Hoffmann, composed of equal parts of steel and whalebone, was not troubled with nerves. (Had he not proved that at Tannenberg when Ludendorff had cracked under the strain?) Within that great shaven skull reposed the most brilliant brain of the German General Staff...*"[129]

Having served with von Schlieffen during the Russo-Japanese war and alongside Hindenburg and Ludendorff during the victorious campaigns on the Eastern Front in 1914, Hoffmann was considered an expert on Russian Affairs. Representatives from Austria-Hungary,Turkey and Bulgaria completed the delegation.

The intentions and attitude of the Russian delegation were immediately outlined at the opening session of the negotiations. Joffe opened by requesting that the proceedings be given full publicity in accordance with the Bolshevik government's rejection of secret diplomacy. He then launching into an address to the people of the belligerent states calling for an end to the war based on the principles outlined in the Decree on Peace. Finally he concluded with three proposals to permit the attainment of an immediate armistice. Firstly the Central Powers were not to transfer troops during the armistice away from the Eastern Front. Secondly the Germans were to evacuate the islands in the Gulf of Riga that had recently been occupied. Lastly, the armistice would have an agreed duration of six months.[130] Considering that the Russian army had virtually disintegrated during the course of 1917 the representatives of the Central Powers were amazed by the confident and optimistic manner in which Joffe was attempting to dictate terms to the Central Powers. This apparent buoyancy on the behalf of the Russian delegation can only be explained in terms of the implicit confidence placed by the Bolsheviks in the conviction that the November revolution would ignite successive waves of concerted action by the European proletariat against the capitalist system. Therefore it was felt that the Central Powers, in an attempt to placate the working classes, would have to accept the Bolshevik terms or risk the consequences. As Trotsky announced in an address to the Petrograd Soviet on November 30 1917:

> *"Under the influence of the masses the German and Austrian Governments have already agreed to put themselves in the dock. You may be sure, comrades, that the prosecutor, in the person of the Russian revolutionary delegation, will be in his place and in due time will make a thunderous speech for the prosecution on the diplomacy of all imperialists."*[131]

Hoffmann regarded the Russian pretensions as humorous rather than formidable. However German policy was based on the need to put an early end to hostilities on the Eastern Front. In order to reach this goal it therefore seemed desirable, at this stage of the negotiations, to reduce to a minimum the conditions to be demanded from the Russians.[132] Therefore in reply to Joffe's opening speech Hoffmann, although aware of the Bolshevik intention to use the negotiations as a platform for propaganda, agreed to the proceedings being publicised on the condition that all records were based on the official minutes.[133] Secondly, Hoffmann offered to conclude a 28 day armistice which could be prolonged if both sides agreed. Finally, although he dismissed the suggestion that his forces should evacuate the islands in the Gulf of Riga, Hoffmann agreed that no further troops would be transferred from the Eastern Front. Hoffmann had little hesitation in agreeing to this latter point, for the agreement was to exempt the vast number of German and Austrian troops who had already received their transfer orders.[134]

When Joffe countered with a proposal that the armistice should be extended to all fronts Hoffmann for the first time referred to the weakness of the position adopted by the Russians by demanding to know by what authority the Russians could speak for the Entente powers. As Hoffmann later noted in his memoirs:

> *"The Russians had to confess that they had no such authority, I therefore proposed that they should keep within the limits of the authority they possessed, and that we should proceed to the negotiation of a separate armistice".*[135]

On the pretext of launching a further plea to the Entente states to participate in the negotiations Joffe returned briefly to Petrograd. However, as Trotsky noted, there was in fact little hope of a favourable response:

> *"Our enemies were quite certain that the whole business was a mere episode, that it was only a question of a day or two, perhaps of a week, and the Soviet Government would be overthrown."*[136]

With the growing appreciation that perhaps they were attempting to overplay a dubious hand, on

December 12 1917, the Bolshevik delegation returned to Brest-Litovsk. Joffe accepted the terms offered but managed to gain agreement on the establishment of limited fraternisation points between the two front lines. In sanctioning this request Hoffmann reasoned:

> "In this way it would be possible to exercise some control, and to intercept the greater part of the propaganda literature that might be expected."[137]

Later events were to indicate that Hoffmann had underestimated the efficiency of the Bolshevik propaganda machinery. However, the German High Command was satisfied with the terms that led to the formal signing of the armistice on December 15 1917. As Ludendorff commented:

> "For the past six months I had devoted myself, and made others devote all their energies, to the attainment of the object we had now achieved."[138]

> "We had some prospect of gaining the final victory."[139]

The advent of an armistice concluded between Russia and the Central Powers threatened once again to taint the Bolshevik government with the suggestion that it was pro-German. In order to disarm this argument the Bolshevik hierarchy immediately placed the responsibility for the signing of a separate armistice at the foot of the Entente powers which had persistently rebuffed the Bolshevik peace proposals. However, privately, Lenin and Trotsky appreciated that, if they were forced into the position of concluding a separate peace with the Central Powers, their bargaining position would not be one of strength. Therefore, their salvation still lay in their prediction of a further series of revolutions throughout Europe. On December 19 1917 Trotsky, in a further appeal to the people of Europe, noted:

"A truly democratic peoples peace will still have to be fought for."[140]

"The Governments opposing peace and the Governments masking aggressive intentions behind talk of peace must be swept away. The workers and soldiers must rest the business of war and peace from the criminal hands of the bourgeoisie and take it into their hands."[141]

It appeared, though, that the Bolsheviks had won a minor victory in that the Central Powers had not specifically rejected their call for a peace based on the principle of no annexations or indemnities. In fact this position seemed in accordance with the Reichstag peace resolution of July 19 1917 which proclaimed:

"Annexations by force and political, economic and financial oppression are incompatible with such a peace."[142]

However, the most significant factor had been that the Imperial Chancellor, Michaelis, had accepted the resolution with the stipulation that it was subject to his own interpretation. In the succeeding months it became increasingly apparent that Michaelis and later his successor, the aging Bavarian Prime Minister, Count von Hertling, under pressure from the Supreme Command, interpreted the resolution as not preventing the acquisition of vast tracts of foreign territory. At the

Crown Council of September 14 1917, Ludendorff made if perfectly clear that the army would not accept peace terms based on anything less than the war aims of 1914 incorporating the annexation of Alsace-Lorraine, parts of Belgium and the creation of Polish, Lithuanian and Courland states closely allied to Germany.[143] In the view of the High Command if puppet governments could be established in these states that approved the creation of close ties with Germany, the situation could not be interpreted as annexation.

In relation to Poland the ambitions of the German generals brought them into direct conflict with Austro-Hungarian ambitions to unite Congress Poland with Austrian Galicia within the Habsburg Empire. However, as Hindenburg stated:

> *"In view of the thoroughly Germanophobe attitudes of the Poles this policy of Austria was pregnant with danger for us."*[144]

In many senses the German Supreme Command was already redrawing the map of Europe to Germany's advantage in preparation for the next war. As Ludendorff noted:

> *"Russia must never again concentrate her armies on the defenceless frontier of East and West Prussia, and never again, with the help of French gold, use the Vistula region as a gate of entry into an unprotected Germany."*[145]

On December 19 1917, in preparation for the forthcoming peace discussions to be held at Brest-Litovsk, the Crown Council met at Kreuznach. Ludendorff outlined that in terms of security, manpower and access to raw materials the domination of Poland and the Baltic states was imperative. In preparation for this policy, in August of 1917, Ludendorff had instructed the military commanders in Lithuania and Courland to establish German sponsored governments within the occupied areas. Furthermore, in December 1917 General Count von Waldersee was appointed head of a newly created office to supervise economic and financial exploitation of the occupied areas. Only the Foreign Minister, Kuhlmann, opposed Ludendorff's ambitious blueprint for the German domination of Eastern Europe. Kuhlmann argued that the permanent incorporation of vast numbers of non-Germanic people within the German state would prove to be counter productive in the long term. While recognising the need for war-time occupation of these areas, Kuhlmann advocated that politically it would be more acceptable to establish, in the post war era, a covert protectorate over Eastern Europe through economic and financial ties rather than blatant annexation. Such was the resolution of both parties that they both left the meeting considering that, although they had not won the day, neither had suffered an emphatic rejection of his proposals. This created a situation that was inevitably to produce confusion and bitter recriminations as the Brest-Litovsk conference unfolded. [147]

The first session of the Brest-Litovsk peace negotiations opened on December 22 1917. The Russian delegation was again led by Joffe with the addition of Pokrovsky and General Samoilo to its previous strength. Baron von Kuhlmann headed the German delegation assisted by Rosenberg and Baron von Hoesch. General

Hoffmann once again represented the Supreme Command while Count Czernin, the Austrian Foreign Minister, arrived from Vienna to defend the interests of the Austro-Hungarian Empire. Bulgaria and Turkey were initially represented by Popoff and Nessimy Bey. However, the Bulgarian Prime Minister, Radoslavov, and the Turkish Grand Vizier, Talaat Pasha, later arrived to assume the leadership of their respective delegations.

The conference commenced with Joffe presenting a six point peace formula based on the points outlined by Lenin on December 8 1917 and approved by the Council of Soviet Commissars on December 10 1917. Firstly, there was not to be any forcible annexation of territory seized during the war and all occupying forces were to be withdrawn at the earliest possible moment. This would permit political independence to be restored to all nations deprived of it during the war. Nationalities which had not possessed political independence before the war were to be allowed to hold plebiscites to determine their future status. Territories inhabited by several nationalities were to devise a legal framework that would allow cultural and national autonomy as far as possible. War indemnities were not to be levied on the belligerent powers although private individuals were to be compensated from a common fund provided by the belligerent nations. All colonial questions were to be determined along the above guidelines. Finally, the use of economic measures to restrict the freedom of small nations was to be condemned.[148]

During the adjournment requested by the Central Powers to consider the Russian proposals, Kuhlmann argued that the Russian formula should be accepted with the proviso that the Central Powers were only committed to carrying out the stated conditions if the Entente nations also joined the negotiations and agreed to the Russian formula.[149] However, as Hoffmann noted, Kuhlmann never at any time had any intention of agreeing to an immediate withdrawal of German troops from the occupied areas of Eastern Europe:

> "...the settlement of the question of the border states, Poland Lithuania and Kurland did not come into the category of annexations, as the legally appointed representatives of these states had decided of their own free will a long time previously, to separate themselves from Russia and to place the settlement of their future status in the hands of Germany or the Central Powers."[150]

Not only did Kuhlmann appreciate the military value of these areas while the war was in progress but also he realised that the East European states could provide a valuable bargaining card if negotiations were opened with the Entente states for a peace settlement.[151] Kuhlmann's immediate priority, though, was to secure a peace settlement with Russia. He therefore agreed to the Russian formula with the stipulation that the Entente nations must also agree knowing full well that the Entente states were unlikely to respond. This in effect would isolate the Bolsheviks and force them into direct negotiations for an immediate separate peace.

Count Czernin was extremely dubious of any suggestion of Austro-Hungarian agreement to the principle of self-determination. However, he supported Kuhlmann's suggestions for he appreciated that not only did the tottering AustroHungarian economy require an agreement granting access to Russian grain supplies, but also the intention of the Entente powers to dismember the Habsburg Empire now bound Austro-Hungary more closely than ever to the pursuit of a military victory in the West advocated by the German Supreme Command[152] Only Hoffmann and, to an extent, the Bulgarian delegate opposed Kuhlmann. From the outset Hoffmann favoured a firm line being taken with the Russians. He proposed that it should be pointed out that the Russians had no authority to speak on behalf of the Entente and therefore there was no need for the charade of awaiting the reaction of the Entente to the conference proposals. Furthermore, he suggested that the German interpretation of what constituted annexation should be made perfectly clear to the Russians.[153] Hoffmann later attempted to justify in his memoirs his eventual agreement to follow Kuhlmann's policy:

> *"As he had gone with the Chancellor of State to G.H.Q. before coming to Brest-Litovsk, I had to suppose that during the consultation of the Supreme Civil Authority and the High Command a decision had been arrived at with regard to the **modus procedendi**, so I had to submit."*[154]

On December 25 1917 Czernin, on behalf of the Central Powers, agreed to the Russian proposals subject to all the belligerent powers adhering to the stated principles of the settlement.[155] As Hoffmann recorded:

> *"The Russians were triumphant and telegraphed their satisfaction to Petrograd. By mutual consent we had now to wait ten days, to give the Entente time to notify if they wished to participate in the Peace Conference."*[156]

In Berlin, though, the news had a mixed reception. While the political parties of the left warmly applauded the German declaration, Ludendorff stated:

"For the future of Germany it was all important that the whole Eastern problem should be solved in a manner which satisfied the interests of Prussia and Germany, and as far as possible removed the danger threatening from Poland."[157]

"The right of self determination was interpreted in a manner that lacked clearness and did not accord with German interests."[158]

"The invitation to the Entente too, could produce nothing but delay. There was no prospect of its being accepted."[159]

Ludendorff instructed Hoffmann to point out to Kuhlmann that he should seek a peace settlement at the earliest possible moment. Furthermore, the Russians should be made aware of the German interpretation of annexation in relation to Courland, Lithuania and Poland.[160]

Although Kuhlmann remained largely unruffled by the remonstrations of the Supreme Command he did concede that the Russians had misunderstood German policy in assuming that, on conclusion of a peace settlement, German forces would retire to the pre-war Eastern frontiers. It was agreed that Hoffmann should point out to Joffe that Germany did not consider it as annexation if the representatives of the Baltic states and Poland elected to associate with Germany. As Hoffmann later noted:

"Joffe looked as if he had received a blow on his head."[161]

The Russians immediately demanded a meeting with Czernin, Kuhlmann and Hoffmann:

"The shock to the Bolsheviks had evidently been a severe one. Indignation mingled with disappointment. Joffe protested, Kamenev stormed, Pokrovsky wept. "How can you talk of peace without annexation", he sobbed, "when nearly eighteen provinces are torn from Russia?"[162]

Kuhlmann and Hoffmann remained impassive but the Russian indignation had deeply perturbed Czernin. Later, in conversation with Kuhlmann, Czernin declared that rather than forfeit the chance of a settlement with Russia, Austro-Hungary would be forced to consider the possibility of a separate treaty with Russia.[163] Although appreciating the need in Vienna for Russian grain, Kuhlmann merely noted Czernin's declaration and asked for written confirmation of its contents. He was well aware that Czernin was unlikely to take any action without German approval. Furthermore, he saw the opportunity to use Czernin's declaration as a valuable weapon if the Supreme Command attempted to increase the pressure on him to bully the Russians into an early and brutal settlement.[164] Hoffmann similarly dismissed the Austrian threat with the comment that a separate peace would assist Germany by releasing troops from the South-Eastern Front with Russia.[165] As Hoffmann commented:

"I could not understand the Count's excitement. In my opinion there was no question of the negotiations

being broken off by the Russians. The Russian masses were longing for peace, the army had crumbled away - it consisted now of mere insubordinate armed hordes - and the only chance the Bolsheviks had of remaining in power was by signing a Peace. They were obliged to accept the conditions of the Central Powers, however hard they might be."[166]

In an attempt to clarify the situation the Russian delegation proposed that their forces would withdraw from Turkey and Persia while German troops withdrew from Courland, Lithuania and Poland to allow unhindered plebiscites to be held to determine the status of those nations. The reply of the Central Powers pointed out that Russia must concede that it had agreed to the principle of self-determination. The governments of the Baltic States had clearly indicated that they desired independence from Russia and association with Germany. There was therefore no need for an immediate evacuation of German troops from the occupied areas.[167] As Wheeler-Bennett noted:

"At last Joffe saw that the optimism which he had displayed in Petrograd after the Armistice and at Brest after the declaration of Christmas Day had been misplaced. Kuhlmann's statement of December 28 had shown beyond all doubting that the original agreement to the formula of "peace without annexations" was but a myth and that the German and Russian conceptions of self-determination were irreconcilable."[168]

At this juncture the conference adjourned to await the official reaction of the Entente powers to the proposals outlined on December 25 1917 and also to permit the delegations to report back to their respective governments. Kuhlmann and Hoffmann received a very mixed reception in Berlin. The socialist wing of the Reichstag, that had so warmly applauded the Christmas declaration, was scathing in its criticism of the German proposals made on December 28 1917. It appeared to them that Kuhlmann was bent on a policy of annexation that ignored the principles incorporated in the Reichstag peace resolution of July 1917. [169] On the other hand, the Supreme Command were disturbed that the German delegation had agreed to an adjournment rather than pressing the Russians to agree immediately to the German terms. Hindenburg refused to contemplate any possibility of plebiscites being held in the occupied states.[170] The wrath of the Supreme command was directed initially against Hoffmann. In his defence, Hoffmann pointed out that it seemed natural to assume that Kuhlmann had based his strategy on a formula agreed by the Crown Council.[171] However, the rift between Hoffmann and the Supreme Command was further exacerbated when, in a private interview with the Kaiser, Hoffmann admitted that he preferred the creation of only marginal alterations to Germany's Eastern Frontiers rather than Ludendorff's advocation of large scale annexations.[172] As Hoffmann argued:

> *"Notwithstanding the measures that Russia had taken, during many decades, we had not been able to manage our fellow-subjects of Polish origin, and I could not see the advantage of any addition to the number of citizens of that nationality."*[175]

However, when the Kaiser reiterated Hoffmann's proposals at the Crown Council meeting at Kreuznach, on January 2 1918, Hindenburg and Ludendorff were outraged not only that Hoffmann should oppose their blueprint but also that the Kaiser should seek the advice of a subordinate officer. The meeting broke up with the Supreme Command agreeing to do no more than report back on the matter.[174] While Ludendorff once again proffered his resignation, Hindenburg in his reply to the Kaiser dated January 7 1918, described Hoffmann's formula as "unacceptable to the General Headquarters" and pointed out that:

> "General Hoffmann is a subordinate and has no responsibility in political matters.
>
> Generally speaking I am bound to ascribe the hitherto unsatisfactory political and economic results to the inadequate preparation for peace negotiations on the part of the Foreign Office and the pliancy of our diplomacy towards our allies and our enemies"[175]

This assault on the ability of the Foreign Office to direct foreign affairs was once again indicative of the conviction held by the military commanders that their role in the formulation of policy was more than just an advisory capacity. As Kitchen noted:

> "They contrived to insist on their right and duty to influence and even decide vital political decisions, all the while insisting that they were offering merely military advice."[176]

In his reply to Hindenburg, on January 12 1917, the Kaiser defended the right of the Foreign Office and the Imperial Chancellory to dictate policy and also pointed out that, in the interests of the wartime alliance, Austro-Hungarian ambitions in Eastern Europe must be taken into consideration. However, while defending Hoffmann and Kuhlmann, the Kaiser bowed to the wishes of the Supreme Command by conceding that the Polish question was still open.[177] The outcome of this brief exchange was that Kuhlmann was able to return to Brest-Litovsk without express instructions to enforce annexations in the East. Hoffmann concluded:

> *"The Privy Council had not settled anything definitely or decisively. The Secretary of State had not been told quite clearly what position he was to take up at Brest, nor had the Polish question been decided. His Majesty, the Kaiser, only approved of what Kuhlmann had done so far, and he had authorised him to continue on the same lines. The difficult problem of the border states remained unsettled."[178]*

The return of the Bolshevik delegation to Petrograd was marked by yet another impassioned plea by Trotsky to the Entente nations to join the negotiations at Brest-Litovsk. Trotsky pointed out that the declaration of the Central Powers on December 25 1917 represented agreement on the restoration of the pre-war frontiers which was a stipulation that the Entente had continually demanded. However, in a resolution placed before the All-Russian Central Executive Committee, Trotsky revealed his disappointment with the German terms:

"We address ourselves to the people of Germany, Austria-Hungary, Bulgaria and Turkey. Under your pressure your governments have been forced in words to appropriate our motto: "No annexations or indemnities", but in fact they are trying to carry on the old policy of annexations. Remember, the conclusion of a speedy and really democratic peace is now more than ever in your hands."[179]

Although Bolshevik strategy still clung to the belief that it was only necessary to accelerate the propaganda programme to precipitate the European revolution, Lenin began to appreciate that perhaps the conditions for revolution in the industrialised states of Western Europe were not as ripe as he had previously believed. In this light it appeared necessary to delay the proceedings at Brest-Litovsk not only to allow time for the European revolutionary forces to mature but also to permit the Bolshevik regime to establish its authority within Russia. Previously, Lenin had not feared German annexationist demands for he was convinced that he would soon be dealing with the representatives of the European proletariat rather than the established hierarchies.[180] However, he was now faced with the prospect of the Central Powers annexing vast areas of Russia and possibly marching on Petrograd to install a puppet regime.

Confronted with the German demands it seemed that Lenin seriously considered breaking off the negotiations and gambling on the escalation of Russia-German conflict to the level of a European revolutionary war. On December 31 1917 Lenin put several questions to the Russian Army Congress concerning the ability of the army to resume the military campaign against the Central Powers.[181] Furthermore, Trotsky discretely sounded the Entente Embassies as to the possibility of receiving military assistance if the struggle against Germany was resumed. Lenin outlined the dilemma of the Bolshevik hierarchy:

> "...should we strive to drag out the peace negotiations, or would a revolutionary abrupt end and immediate rupture of peace negotiations, because of the German annexationist policy, be preferable as a decisive and firm step which would prepare the ground for a possible revolutionary war?"[182]

In reality, given the disintegration of the Russian army as an effective fighting force, only one option was possible. Trotsky was appointed head of the Russian delegation with express instructions to prolong the negotiations with the Central Powers. He immediately opened his campaign with a proposal that the negotiations be transferred to a neutral country.[183] However, the weakness of the Russian standpoint was clearly apparent for when the Central Powers replied with a threat to denounce the Armistice the Russian delegation had no option but to set out once again for the bleak fortress of Brest-Litovsk.

When the delegations from the Central Powers returned to Brest-Litovsk in January 1918 it was soon apparent that the unity of purpose that had marked the earlier session of the conference was somewhat tarnished. Kuhlmann was painfully aware not only of the fragility of domestic support for his policy but also of the clash of ambitions between Germany and Austria-Hungary concerning the future status of

Poland. Czernin was increasingly pre-occupied with the need for the early conclusion of an agreement to grant the Habsburg Empire access to the grain supplies of the Ukraine, while Hoffmann appreciated that some form of agreement was imperative if troops were to be released from the Eastern Front to bolster the planned Spring offensive in the West. On January 9 1918 in an effort to clarify the position, as they saw it, Kuhlmann and Czernin opened the conference by pointing out that, as the Entente nations had ignored the invitations to join the negotiations ,the Central Powers considered the declaration of December 25 1917 to be invalid and therefore Russia must confine itself to discussion of a separate peace.[184] Trotsky countered by stating that Russia could not accept the German interpretation of self-determination and that only after a withdrawal of all occupying forces could truly representative governments be elected in the Baltic Sates. Kuhlmann retaliated with the assertion that the occupied territories had already elected governments which had freely declared their intention to associate with Germany. There was therefore no suggestion of, or need for, troop withdrawals from the Baltic States.[185] Almost immediately Trotsky had succeeded in forcing Kuhlmann to lay his cards on the table. At last it appeared that Kuhlmann had come up against an opponent who could match his dialectics and a stalemate threatened to arise. As Hoffmann noted:

"Trotsky was certainly the most interesting personality in the new Russian Government: clever, versatile, cultivated, possessed of great energy, powers of work, and eloquence, he gave the impression of a man who knew exactly what he

*wanted and who would not be deterred from using
any means for attainment of his end."* [186]

The unexpected prolongation of discussions exasperated Count Czernin and General Hoffmann. Wheeler-Bennett observed:

"The nerves of the Austrian Foreign Minister became frayed. To have to listen day by day to these seemingly endless "spiritual wrestling matches" while the sands of his country's life were running out, reduced him to a state of almost hysterical prostration. Daily, the news from Vienna and Budapest grew worse; almost hourly, the slim margin between possible victory and certain defeat shrank more and more." [187]

Although Hoffmann initially believed that Trotsky sincerely wanted to conclude peace, as the negotiations appeared to be approaching a deadlock, he increasingly suspected that the Bolshevik delegation was primarily using the conference as a platform for propaganda. [188] On January 12 1918, in reply to Kamenev's demand that the Central Powers renounce all annexationist ambitions in the occupied states, Hoffmann bluntly pointed out that the Bolsheviks had themselves violated the principle of self determination in their campaigns to break up the National Assemblies formed by the White Russians and the Ukrainians. In conclusion, Hoffmann asserted:

"...that the question of the border states was settled, as far as the German G.H.Q. was concerned: they took the view that the legal representatives of these

states had decided on separation from Soviet Russia, and no further vote was necessary."[189]

This attempt to restore a measure of reality to the proceedings had been sanctioned by Kuhlmann in order to placate the Supreme Command. However, although Hoffmann considered that he had paved the way for a breakthrough in the negotiations, Kuhlmann argued that the abrupt approach adopted by Hoffmann had in fact been counter-productive in that it displayed German intentions as being blatantly annexationist.[190] Kuhlmann was under no illusion that Trotsky would forfeit this opportunity to increase the stream of propaganda already flowing out of Petrograd.

While Kuhlmann still considered that the Bolsheviks could be brought to voluntarily accept his terms, Hoffmann and Czernin, almost in desperation, turned to a new line of approach.

On January 7 1918 a delegation from the Ukrainian Rada in Kiev had arrived at Brest-Litovsk claiming to represent the Ukrainian state established following the Bolshevik declaration of the right to self-determination for the various national entities within the former Tsarist Empire. The Bolsheviks received the delegation with barely concealed hostility for the Rada was dominated by liberal elements which the Bolsheviks were actively attempting to overthrow through the agency of a Bolshevik sponsored rival Ukrainian regime based in Kharkov. However, the delegation was warmly welcomed at Brest-Litovsk by the representatives of the Central Powers. As Hoffmann recorded:

"Kuhlmann and I received the Ukrainians with pleasure as their appearance offered a possibility of

playing   them   off   against   the   Petrograd   Delegation."[191]

Hoffmann now opened informal discussions with the Ukrainians concerning the possibility of concluding a peace treaty between the Ukraine and the Central Powers. It was considered that not only would this provide the Central Powers with access to Ukrainian grain supplies but also it would force Trotsky to appreciate that, unless he came to terms with the Central Powers in the near future, bilateral agreements would be concluded with the Russian border states irrespective of the attitude adopted by the Bolshevik regime.[192] The success of the negotiations hinged essentially on the stance assumed by the Austro-Hungarian delegation. Czernin was well aware that in exchange for coming to an agreement with the Central Powers the Ukrainians would insist that the Polish district of Cholm be ceded to the Ukraine while the Austro-Hungarian districts of Galicia and Bukovinia be formed into an independent crownland within the Austro-Hungarian Empire. To agree to such conditions would effectively destroy any hope of gaining Polish support for the establishment of Polish state under Austro-Hungarian patronage. Furthermore, the establishment of a Galician crownland would represent a concession to the principle of self-determination that threatened to dissolve the remaining ties that united the Habsburg Empire.[193] However, the dependence of the tottering Austro-Hungarian economy on German grain supplies had already deprived Czernin of the ability to further threaten Kuhlmann with the prospect of a separate peace settlement with the Russians if an overall agreement was not soon forthcoming. On January 17 Czernin received a message from the Emperor Karl:

"I must once more earnestly impress upon you that the whole fate of the monarchy and of the dynasty depends on peace being concluded at Brest-Litovsk as soon as possible."[194]

"If peace be not made at Brest, there will be a revolution here, be there ever so much to eat. This is a serious instruction at a serious time."[195]

Such was the desperation in the reports from Vienna and Budapest[196] that on January 18 1918 Czernin informed Hoffmann that he would agree to the Ukrainian terms.

Faced with the immediate prospect of a separate peace between the Central Powers and the Ukraine and appreciating that his opponents were unlikely to tolerate any further major delay of the negotiations, Trotsky requested a short adjournment in order to return to Petrograd to consult the Bolshevik hierarchy. On the same day that Trotsky set out for Petrograd, Bolshevik troops forcibly dispersed the first meeting of the Constituent Assembly. Previously, Lenin had used the demand for the creation of the Assembly as a lever against the Provisional Government. Now that the Provisional Government had been overthrown, the Bolsheviks revealed their true colours and ruthlessly set about suppressing any group or organisation, irrespective of its legitimacy, that threatened the supreme authority of the Bolshevik party. The events of January 18 and 19 had repercussions on an international scale. The apparent disregard of the Bolsheviks for the principles of democracy threatened to severely undermine the stance that had been assumed at Brest-Litovsk. Furthermore, the fact that the Bolsheviks seemed to be purging all domestic opposition aroused suspicions throughout Europe that all opponents of a separate peace were being eliminated in preparation for the settlement with the Germans that the Bolshevik leadership appeared to have been moving steadily towards.

It was amid this rash of speculation that the Central Committee of the Bolshevik Party met on January 21 1918 to consider their future policy. The division within the inner hierarchy was plainly revealed. In opposition to the German demands Bukharin advocated the immediate declaration of a revolutionary war to which, he claimed, the European proletariat would soon rally. Trotsky repeated his conviction that the German terms were unacceptable. He argued that if Russia simply declared that it had withdrawn from the war but had not accepted the German terms, there was little that the German government could do about it for the German working classes would actively prevent the resumption of a military offensive to crush the Russian revolutionary government.[197] In view of the disintegration of the Russian army and the absence of positive indications of an imminent revolution in Western Europe only Lenin was boldly prepared to face the facts. He pointed out that the challenge to the Bolshevik government from organised political forces within Russia was just as great as the challenge from the Central Powers:

> "...for the success of socialism in Russia a certain amount of time, ... , will be necessary, during which

the hands of the Socialist Government must be absolutely free for the job of vanquishing the bourgeoisie in our country first, and of arranging widespread and far-reaching mass organisational work." [198]

The Bolshevik government was confronted with a virtual ultimatum from the German government:

"The Socialist Government of Russia is faced with the question - a question which brooks no postponement - of whether to accept this annexationist peace now, or at once to wage a revolutionary war. Actually speaking, no middle course exists."[199]

But the question of whether it is possible to wage a revolutionary war "now and at once" must be decided exclusively from the standpoint of whether material conditions permit it and of the interest of the socialist revolution which has already begun.[200]

Pointing to the exhaustion of the army and the absence of definite indications of a revolution in Western Europe, Lenin argued against the declaration of a revolutionary war and in favour of a separate peace:

"In concluding a separate peace we free ourselves as much as is possible at the present moment from both hostile imperialist groups, we take advantage of their mutual enmity and warfare which hamper concerted action on their part against us, and for a certain period have our hands free to advance and to consolidate the socialist revolution."[201]

Lenin agreed that a revolutionary war remained as the ultimate goal of the Bolshevik regime but attacked any premature action that would result in the destruction of the Russian revolutionary movement.

Although based on a sound appreciation of the situation the extent to which the Bolshevik hierarchy adhered to the belief that the international revolution was imminent was indicated by the fact that, when put to the vote, Bukharin's resolution received 32 votes as opposed to 16 for Trotsky and 15 for Lenin. At a further meeting of the Central Executive Committee the following day Lenin once again pleaded his case:

"Germany is only pregnant with revolution. The second month must not be mistaken for the ninth. But here in Russia we have a, lusty child. We may kill it if we start a war."[202]

In an attempt to salvage the essence of his policy and to avoid a major division within the party, Lenin agreed to support Trotsky's formula of "No war - No peace" in return for agreement that Trotsky would oppose the launching of a revolutionary war. In this form Trotsky's resolution was carried by the Central Committee and a form of compromise had been achieved.[203]

It would seem that the optimism displayed by Trotsky was based largely on reports from Berlin and Vienna that strikes had broken out and that the working class at last appeared determined to dictate terms to their respective governments. However, while the armed forces remained loyal the revolutionary movement failed to seriously challenge the authority of the Government and by February 3 1917 most areas of dissent had been ruthlessly suppressed. Against this background Kuhlmann reported to Hindenburg, Ludendorff and von Hertling on the progress made at Brest-Litovsk. The Supreme Command considered that Kuhlmann had allowed Trotsky to outmanoeuvre him and delay the conclusion of a settlement. As Ludendorff noted:

> *"Peace was not delayed by our demands but merely by the revolutionary aims of the Bolsheviks and by want of resolution in our delegates, as well as by the attitude of Germany and Austria where the people, being ignorant of the world, did not understand the inner meaning of the Russian Revolution."*[204]

As evidence of their pressing need to conclude a treaty with Russia before launching the Spring offensive in the West, for the first time, the Supreme Command appeared ready to reduce their annexationist stipulations in the East. Hindenburg proposed that the frontier with Russia be re-drawn approximately midway between the line advocated by Ludendorff in December and that proposed by Hoffmann to the Kaiser. In return Kuhlmann was to bring the negotiations to an early conclusion.[205] Once again, with the tacit support of Hertling, Kuhlmann avoided a direct acceptance of the conditions outlined by the Supreme Command. However, as he returned to Brest-Litovsk, he fully appreciated that he could not resist indefinitely the increasing pressure to deliver an ultimatum to the Russians.

With the resumption of the conference Trotsky immediately sensed that the representatives of the

Central Powers seemed to have recaptured a unity of purpose. Wheeler-Bennett commented:

"For the first time since the conference opened, the delegates of the Central Powers were as one in their desire to achieve a decision with all decent speed and to bring finally to an end the tragic comedy of the past six weeks."[206]

Immediately, Trotsky produced his trump card in the form of a delegation claiming to represent the Ukrainian Soviet Government. In pointing out that the Ukrainian Soviet forces now controlled vast areas of the Ukraine, Trotsky ridiculed the legitimacy of the Rada representatives:

"...hinting that the power of the Central Rada had vanished and that its representatives could look upon their room in Brest-Litovsk as the only space of which they had any right to dispose."[207]

Hoffmann was forced to concede privately that Trotsky was correct:

"Bolshevism was advancing victoriously, the Central Rada and Ukrainian Provisional Government had fled."[208]

However, Kuhlmann and Czernin were not to be sidetracked by this blatant attempt to block the proposed treaty with the Ukraine. Of the military situation Hoffmann agreed:

"The difficulties were transitory in so far as any time we could support the Government with arms and establish it again."[209]

Furthermore, Czernin, on his recent visit to Vienna, had received express instructions to conclude a treaty with the Ukrainian Rada.[210] As Czernin noted in his diary on January 30 1918 he doubted that a treaty could be agreed with the Bolsheviks:

"There is no doubt that the revolutionary happenings in Austria and in Germany have enormously raised the hopes of the Petersburgers for a general convulsion, and it seems to me altogether out of the question now to come to any peace terms with the Russians."[211]

Accordingly, Czernin identified his main priority as the establishment of a treaty with the Ukraine which would give the Austrians access to desperately needed supplies of grain. Therefore, on February 1 1918 Trotsky was informed that the Central Powers had no intention of altering their recognition of the Ukrainian Rada as the legitimate representative of the Ukrainian state.

At this juncture the conference was adjourned for three days to allow Kuhlmann and Czernin to return to Berlin for a planned conference on the conduct of the war. The conference immediately indicated the growing area of dissension between the two allies, as Czernin recorded:

"I had several violent passages of arms with Ludendorff."[212]

*"Apart from deciding on our tactics for Brest, we have at last to set down **in writing** that we are only obliged to fight for the pre-war possessions of Germany. Ludendorff was violently opposed to this*

and said, "If Germany makes peace without profit, then Germany has lost the war."[213]

The Supreme Command were exasperated at Czernin's efforts to seek a settlement with the Entente that was not based on large scale annexations that would improve their strategic position in any future conflict.[214] As Hindenburg noted of Czernin:

"His political plans were directed far more to efforts to avoid disaster than to make full use of our victories."[215]

However, agreement was reached on the format of a settlement with the Ukraine and, that following the signing of this treaty, an ultimatum should be delivered to the Russians.[216]

With the return of the delegates to Brest-Litovsk, Czernin made a last attempt to find a compromise between the German and Russian standpoints. Trotsky, though, proved to be evasive on most points and openly condemned the proposed treaty with the Ukraine.[217] When on February 7 1918 it was revealed that Bolshevik propaganda had urged the German troops to mutiny and murder the Kaiser and his military leaders, Czernin could only conclude:

"The dastardly behaviour of these Bolsheviks renders negotiation impossible. I cannot blame Germany for being incensed at such proceedings."[218]

Hoffmann warned Kuhlmann that the Supreme Command would brook no further delay, while an angry telegram from the Kaiser instructed Kuhlmann to break off negotiations with the declaration that

Germany intended to occupy Courland, Lithuania, Livonia and Estonia.[219]

On February 9 1918 the treaty with the Ukraine was finally signed with the pledge by the Rada representatives that approximately one million tons of grain would be made available for the Central Powers. The following day Kuhlmann prepared to confront Trotsky with the German peace terms. However, the representatives of the Central Powers were taken aback when Trotsky declared:

> *"In the name of the Council of Peoples' Commissars, the Government of the Russian Federal Republic informs the Governments and peoples united in war against us, the Allied and neutral countries, that, in refusing to sign a peace of annexation, Russia declares, on its side, the state of war with Germany, Austria-Hungary, Turkey and Bulgaria as ended."[220]*

> *"The Russian troops are receiving at the same time an order for a general demobilisation on all lines of the fronts."[221]*

As Hoffmann recorded:

> *"The whole congress sat speechless when Trotsky had finished his declaration. We were all dumbfounded."[222]*

Confident that a negotiated settlement could not have been achieved on terms satisfactory to the Bolshevik government and that the German people would not allow the Russian revolutionary movement to be crushed, Trotsky had played his last card. That night the Russian delegation left Brest-Litovsk considering that they had engineered a major coup. Trotsky's optimism was reinforced by reports from German sources:

"Professor Kriege, adviser to the German delegation, told one of our delegates that in the present conditions there could be no question of a new German offensive against Russia. Count Mirbach, then at the head of the German Mission in Russia, left for Berlin assuring us that a satisfactory agreement on the exchange of prisoners had been reached."[223]

Trotsky's hopes were not entirely unfounded. At Brest-Litovsk the reaction of the delegations of the Central Powers was of almost unanimous relief that peace had at last materialised. Furthermore, Germany retained the occupied areas of Eastern Europe without the blatant stigma of an annexationist treaty.[224] In Vienna the news was greeted with wild celebrations. However, it was significant that the one dissenting voice at Brest-Litovsk was that of General Hoffmann:

"We had made an Armistice with Russia with the object of arranging the terms of peace. If peace were not concluded the object of the Armistice was not attained and therefore the Armistice came automatically to an end, and hostilities recommenced. Trotsky's declaration was, in my opinion, nothing more than a denunciation of the Armistice."[225]

On February 13 1918 Kuhlmann, Hertling, the Kaiser and the Supreme Commanders met at Homburg.

The attitude of the Supreme Command was outlined by Hindenburg:

> "In this attitude of Trotsky, which simply flouted all international principles, I could see nothing but an attempt to keep the situation in the East in a state of perpetual suspense."[226]

Ludendorff moved immediately to the heart of the matter:

> "We could not possibly leave matters in this condition. At any moment fresh dangers might arise while we were fighting for our lives in the West.[227] Our military and food situation required that the Armistice should be denounced, the position in the East definitely cleared up, and rapid action taken."[228]

In order to release troops for the Western Front Ludendorff demanded that the Eastern Front be stabilised by the launching of a military campaign to force the Russians to concede to the German terms. Furthermore, Ludendorff pointed out the undeniable need for unrestricted access to Ukrainian grain and the danger that an undefeated Bolshevik state might possibly resume the struggle against the Central Powers with aid from Britain and the United States.[229] Faced with these arguments, Hertling capitulated to the demands of the Supreme Command. However, Kuhlmann stood firm in his conviction that the resumption of hostilities would severely test the alliance with Austria-Hungary and the loyalty of the domestic population. He proposed that Germany should accept the status quo for a permanent settlement with Russia could always be achieved after the war in the West had been won.[230]Despite Kuhlmann's resistance, the arguments of the Supreme Command won the day.[231] Although the Kaiser refused to sanction a full scale assault on Russia to oust the Bolsheviks, as some of the military commanders would have liked, [232] orders were issued for a limited advance to consolidate the German hold on Estonia, Livonia and the Ukraine.

With the receipt of these instructions, Hoffmann resumed the offensive against the Russian forces on February 13 1918. Despite impassioned pleas by the Bolshevik leadership to the Russian Army to resist the German forces, within a matter of days Hoffmann's troops swept through Estonia and Livonia.[233] On February 20 Hoffmann observed in his diary:

> "The Russian Army is more rotten than I had supposed. There is no fight left in them, Yesterday one lieutenant with six men took six hundred Cossack prisoners."[234]

> "Indeed in many sectors of the frontline wholesale desertions left only a handful of officers to resist the Germans."

The news of this advance was a shattering blow to Trotsky and the faction that clung to the belief that an assault upon revolutionary Russia would precipitate revolution in the West. At a meeting of the Bolshevik Central Committee Lenin drew on his pledge from Trotsky not to support a revolutionary war and narrowly gained acceptance of a resolution agreeing to the German terms:

*"If the Germans should demand the overturn of the
Bolshevik Government, then, of course, we would
have to fight. All other demands can and should be
granted."*[235]

*"Even if we give up Finland, Livonia and Estonia,
we still retain the Revolution. I recommend that we
sign the peace terms offered to us by the Germans. If
they should demand that we keep out of the affairs of
the Ukraine, Livonia and Estonia, we shall have to
accept those terms too."*[236]

A wireless message accepting the German terms
was dispatched. However, Hoffmann's initial response
was to demand that written confirmation of the
message should be presented to the German military
headquarters in the East. Undoubtedly Hoffmann
considered that he had no intention of missing the
opportunity to advance deep into Russian territory by
rushing to conclude a settlement with the Bolsheviks.
On February 23 1918 the Germans presented their terms
to the Bolsheviks. The ultimatum was far harsher than
the original terms outlined at Brest-Litovsk. Not only
was Russia to lose the Baltic provinces but also
Courland, Finland and the Ukraine. Furthermore, an
undertaking was demanded to demobilise the Russian
Army and cease all propaganda activity in the areas to
be surrendered.[237]

These terms were bitterly received in Petrograd. The
Left Socialist Revolutionaries advocated accepting aid
from the Entente to continue the war against the
Central Powers. In fact Trotsky, fearing that the
Germans were determined to overthrow the Bolshevik
regime, had already contacted the representatives of the

Entente powers in Petrograd concerning the possibility of military aid being resumed.[238] However, Lenin, after pointing out that the Russian Army had evaporated, concluded:

> "...that the policy of the "revolutionary phrase" was over as far as he was concerned and that if it were continued he would resign his government and central committee posts. He insisted that the Soviets must buy time with territory."[239]

By a margin of seven votes to four, with four abstentions, the Central Committee accepted Lenin's resolution and later the same evening the Petrograd Soviet and Central Executive Committee of the Congress of Soviets reluctantly ratified this decision although Bukharin and his followers subsequently resigned from the party.[240]

Following their acceptance of the German terms, the Bolsheviks were instructed to dispatch a further delegation to Brest-Litovsk to sign the treaty. As Hoffmann noted:

> "The negotiations here will last three to four days at the most, as this time the Comrades must simply swallow what we put before them."[241]

Hoffmann could barely conceal his satisfaction with the peace terms:

> "It must be admitted that the Foreign Office and G.H.Q. have worked well together. It contains everything we ought to insist on."[242]

On March 1 1913 negotiations were once again opened at Brest-Litovsk. However, the dramatic change in the status of the discussions was indicated by the fact that Kuhlmann, Czernin and Trotsky chose not to attend. Although the Central Powers added yet a further stipulation, in demanding that Russia cede Batum, Kars and Ardahan to Turkey, the head of the Russian delegation, Sokolnikov, refused to enter into any discussion of the terms. Sokolnikov declared:

> "The peace which is now being signed at Brest-Litovsk is not a peace based on the voluntary agreement of the peoples of Russia, Germany, Austria-Hungary, Bulgaria and Turkey. It is a peace dictated at the point of the sword. It is a peace which revolutionary Russia is compelled to accept with its teeth clenched."[243]

In reply to a bitter attack by the Moscow Regional Bureau of the Bolshevik Party on the signing of the peace and the betrayal of the European proletariat, Lenin observed:

> "...The interest of the international revolution demand that the Soviet power, having overthrown the bourgeoisie in our country, should **help** that revolution, but that it should choose a **form** of help which is commensurate with its own strength."[244]

> "... to refuse to conclude even the vilest peace when you have no army would be a reckless gamble."[245]

> "We shall not perish even from a dozen obnoxious peace treaties if we take revolt seriously. No conquerors can destroy us if we do not destroy ourselves by despair and phrase-making."[246]

Given just two weeks to ratify the terms of the treaty, on March 6 1918, Lenin confronted the Seventh Congress of the Bolshevik Party and vociferous opposition to the peace terms from a large and influential group formed around Bukharin, Radek and Dybenko. Lenin immediately turned to an assault on those who advocated the launching of a revolutionary war:

*"... to prate in the face of this panicky flight of the army - not one detachment of which was **stopped** by the advocates of revolutionary war - is downright shameful."*[247]

Faced with the disintegration of the army and Lenin's allusion to Prussia's dramatic recovery from the Tilsit Peace of 1807, the Congress agreed to ratify the treaty. This ratification was confirmed by the All-Russian Congress of Workmens' Soldiers' and Peasants' Deputies on March 16 1918. Certainly Lenin was under no illusion that if the treaty was not ratified the German Army would spurn the opportunity to crush the Bolshevik regime. This opinion was confirmed by Hoffmann in his memoirs:

"We are waiting to see if Russia will duly ratify the Peace - they must do so within a fortnight. Otherwise we shall certainly march on Petersburg".

With the ratification of the treaty of Brest-Litovsk it appeared that the Central Powers had achieved a major victory with the withdrawal of Russia from the war. Furthermore, the power and influence of the Supreme Command within Germany was at its zenith. The terms presented to the Bolsheviks represented an emphatic victory for Ludendorff and Hindenburg over their persistent adversary Kuhlmann. Under the guise of military operations to secure access to the desperately needed grain and war materials of Eastern Europe, the Supreme Command had succeeded in redrawing the frontiers of Eastern Europe in a manner that encompassed the acquisition of vast tracts of territory that had been advocated by the military throughout the war.[249] The intellectual acrobatics of the German Social Democratic Party in ratifying the treaty of Brest-Litovsk only served to underline the capitulation of the German government to the virtual military dictatorship.[250] After the signing of the treaty, even Kuhlmann was forced to concede that:

> "One could probably say that the Eastern sky was beginning to lighten, but it would perhaps be better not, as yet, to assume that the transfer from war on two fronts to war on a single front is definitely assured."[251]

Indeed the underlying principle of the treaty had been the German acceptance that peace could only be achieved in the West through force of arms. Therefore, it was necessary to end the war in the East so that the entire resources of the Central Powers could be deployed in an offensive against Britain and France. However, despite the signing of the treaty of Brest-Litovsk, the German and Austro-Hungarian armies were forced to mount extensive military campaigns in the Baltic states and the Ukraine, which required the commitment of over one million soldiers, before these areas could be placed firmly under German control.[252]

Furthermore, although Czernin claimed that grain from the Ukraine saved the lives of millions of people within the Austro-Hungarian Empire,[253] the Central Powers were only able to extract little more than one tenth of the grain that the Ukrainian Rada had promised to supply in March 1918.[254] The problems facing the German military authorities in the Ukraine were not only those of extracting grain from a hostile and war weary local populace but also the disruption created by frequent harassment of the German forces by armed Bolshevik factions. Hindenburg was forced to admit:

"It was absolutely necessary for us to leave behind strong German forces in the East, if only to maintain a barrier between Bolshevist armies and the land we had liberated."[255]

In the summer of 1918 it would appear that the German Supreme Command seriously considered mounting a military campaign to oust the Bolshevik government that had now been transferred to Moscow. However, the reasons why this project was eventually rejected, as it had been in September 1917 and February 1918, were essentially twofold. Firstly, the Supreme Command considered that the future of the war hinged on the success or failure of the Spring offensive in the West. The problem of settling any outstanding differences with Russia was of secondary importance. Therefore, once a peace settlement had been established on the Eastern Front German forces were transferred on a large scale to France leaving little scope or provision for a further campaign against Russia. Secondly, German support for the Bolshevik party had been based on the recognition of mutual interest in Russia's withdrawal from the war. If the Bolsheviks were now deposed a serious political vacuum could have developed within Russia that might have been filled by a political faction advocating a resumption of the war. The German Foreign Ministry was aware that there would be no shortage of financial and material assistance from the Entente nations for such a movement. With these considerations in mind the German Foreign Ministry chose to continue to provide the Bolshevik regime with considerable financial support during the Spring and Summer of 1918. This was illustrated by a report from the German Minister in Moscow, Mirbach, to the German Foreign Ministry on May 16 1918:

> "I am still trying to counter efforts of the Entente and support the Bolsheviks However, I would be grateful for instructions as to whether overall situation justifies use of larger sums in our interests if necessary..."[256]

The following day Kuhlmann replied:

> "Please use larger sums as it is greatly in our interests that Bolsheviks should survive."[257]

German policy can only really be interpreted in the light that it was directed by the military to the attainment of the short term goal of achieving a military victory in the West. The nebulous ambition to establish a political and economic hegemony over Eastern Europe almost completely failed to take account of the political virulence of the Bolshevik creed. Although it was appreciated that Bolshevism represented a direct challenge to the continued existence of the German

Imperial state, the Kaiser's vague notion that after the Bolshevik state had served its purpose it would be simple to engineer a military coup to restore the rule of the Russian aristocracy, exemplified the failure of the German ruling classes to appreciate the danger inherent within a class based revolutionary doctrine.[258]

The absence of any form of genuine Russo-German understanding was indicated by Lenin's terse reaction when presented with the final draft of the Brest-Litovsk treaty:

> "What, not only do you want me to sign this imprudent peace treaty, but also to read it? No, no, never! I shall neither read it nor carry out its terms whenever there is a chance not to do so."[259]

The Bolshevik attitude to the treaty was entirely pragmatic. Peace with the Central Powers was essential to reduce the likelihood of the Bolshevik government being overthrown by either the German army or the Russian people. The Bolsheviks had ridden to power on the basis of their pledge to end the war. Lenin appreciated that to retain power he must fulfill that pledge. To achieve this goal he was literally prepared to pay almost any price in terms of territory and undertakings short of surrendering Bolshevik rule within Russia. As Trotsky noted:

> "We must not let this opportunity slip by. The well-being of the Revolution was the supreme law! We must accept the peace which we dared not refuse; we must gain some time for intensive work in the interior, including the reconstruction of our army."[260]

In order to engineer and later to defend the Bolshevik revolution Lenin had no scruples concerning the acceptance of financial assistance from Germany. Therefore, the strange alliance of two regimes that were direct opposites in terms of their origins and their ambitions was constructed on the recognition of a mutual interest in the ending of the war in Eastern Europe. However, the distance between Moscow and Berlin was extensive, not only in the geographic sense but also in terms of their respective outlooks on the format of post-war European society. Given this intrinsic clash of long term interests it appeared that the tacit Russo-German understanding was built on shifting sands and could be little more than transitory.

References

1. Louis L Snyder, **Historic Documents of World War One** (New York, 1958) pp. 30-33.

2. Martin Kitchen, **The Silent Dictatorship** (London, 1977) p. 18.

3. **Ibid., loc.cit**

4. Z A B Zeman, **A Diplomatic History of the First World War** (London, 1971) p. 83.

5. Walter Hubatsch, **Germany and the Central Powers in the World War. 1914-18** (Kansas, 1963) p. 86.

6. Frank A Golder, **Documents of Russian History. 1914-17** (Gloucester, Mass, 1964) p. 48

7. Ibid., pp. 41-47

8. Snyder, p.117

9. Zeman, p. 88

10. Gerhard Schulz, **Revolutions and Peace Treaties** (London, 1972) pp. 45-46.

11. Zeman, p. 91.

12. Z A B **Zeman,Germany and the Revolution in Russia 1915-18** (hereafter cited as Zeman **G R R**) Minister in Bern to the Chancellor, A28659, 30.9.1915, pp. 6-7.

13. Ibid., loc.cit.

14. Zeman, p. 95.

15. Zeman **G R R.**, pp. 1-2, A934, Under Secretary of State to State Secretary, 9.1.1915.

16. Ibid., p. 2 A1451, State Secretary to Foreign Ministry, 13.1.1915.

17. Ibid., p. 3.

18. Ibid., p. 10, AS6213, State Secretary to Minister in Copenhagen, 26.12.1915.

19. Zeman, pp. 101-102.

20. Zeman, **G R R.**, pp. 14-15, AS293, Minister in Copenhagen to the Chancellor, 23.1.1916.

21. Ibid., p. 92.

22. John W Wheeler-Bennett, **Brest Litovsk. The Forgotten Peace** (London, 1966) p.100.

23. Kitchen, p. 22.

24. General Ludendorff, **The General Staff and its Problems**,Volume II, (London, 1920) pp. 491-98.

25. Schulz, p.14.

26. **Ibid.**, p. 13.

27. **Ibid.**, pp. 34-35.

28. **Ibid.**, p. 25.

29. **Ibid.**, pp. 30-31.

30. Hubatsch, pp. 87-80

31. Ludendorff, **The General Staff. Vol II**, pp. 414-42.

32. **Ibid.**, pp. 420-25.

33. Zeman, p.113.

34. Schulz, p.28.

35. **Ibid., loc.cit**

36. Ludendorff, **The General Staff, Vol I**, pp. 283-84

37. Marshall von Hindenburg, **Out of My Life** (London, 1933), p.169

38. Zeman, p.116.

39. **Ibid., loc.cit.**

40. **Ibid.**, p. 120.

41. Ludendorff, **The General Staff. Vol I**, pp. 299-303.

42. **Ibid.**, pp. 304-6.

43. Hubatsch, pp. 87-88

44. **Ibid.**, p. 88.

45. Golder, pp. 51-53.

46. General A A Brussilov, **A Soldier's Notebook. 1914-18** (London, 1930), p. 282.

47. Golder, p. 51.

48. General Ludendorff, **My War Memories. Vol I** (London, 1919), p.401.

49. **Ibid.**, pp. 396-99

50 Zeman, p. 100.

51 Wheeler-Bennett, p.11

52. **Ibid.**, pp. 11-12.

53. **Ibid.**, pp. 12-13.

54. **Ibid.**, p. 13.

55. **Ibid.**, p. 23.

56. **Ibid.**, pp. 23-24.

57. **Ibid.**, p. 24.

58. Golder, pp. 323-24.

59. **Ibid.**, pp. 311-12.

60. Schulz, pp. 65-6.

61. Golder., pp. 325-29.

62. **Izvestia**, 31.3.1917. Quoted in Zeman, p. 211.

63. Golder, pp. 329-31.

64. Golder, pp. 333-34.

65. **Ibid.**, pp. 353-55.

66. **Ibid.**, pp. 340-43.

67. **Ibid., loc.cit.**

68. Leon Trotsky, **The History of the Russian Revolution to Brest Litovsk** (London, 1919) p13.

69. Zeman, p. 212.

70. Brussilov, pp. 306-7

71. Hindenburg, p. 197.

72. **Ibid.**, p. 198.

73. Ludendorff, **My War Memories. Vol II**, p.413.

73. **Ibid.**, p. 432.

74. General Max Hoffmann, **War Memoirs. Vol II** (London, 1928), p. 179.

75. Zeman, p. 97

76. Zeman **G R R** , pp. 30-31, AS1273, Minister in Copenhagen to Foreign Ministry, 2.4.1917. Also Zeman **G R R** pp. 23-4.

77. **Ibid.**, pp. 24-25, AS1125, State Secretary to Foreign Ministry Liaison Officer at General Headquarters, 23.3.1917.

78. Schulz, p. 53.

79. **Ibid.**, p. 63.

80. David Shub, **Lenin A Biography**, (London, .1977), pp 208-9.

81. **Ibid.**, p. 209.

82. Zeman **G R R**, pp. 35-6, AS13O1, Minister in Bern to Foreign Ministry, 4.4.1917.

83 **Ibid.**, pp. 38-9, AS1317, Minister in Bern to Chancellor 5.4.1917.

Ibid., pp. 39-40, AS1322, Minister in Bern to Foreign Ministry, 6.4.1917.

84. Ibid., p. 40, AS1317, Under State Secretary to Minister in Bern 7.4.1917.

85. Hill & Mudie, **The Letters of Lenin** (London, 1937) p.425.

86 Ibid., p. 429.

87 Ibid., p. 430.

88 Shub, p.247.

89 Hill & Mudie, p.424.

90 Shub, p.427.

91 Ibid., loc.cit.

92 Zeman **G R R** pp. 70-71, AS3640, State Secretary to the Foreign Ministry Liaison Officer at Imperial Court to the Foreign Ministry, 21.4.1917.

93 Ibid., loc.cit.to Minister in Copenhagen, 18.8.1917.

94 Ibid. p.51, A12976, Foreign Ministry Liaison Officer at Imperial Court to Foreign Ministry, 21.4.1917.

95 Ibid. p.69, A26509, Under State Secretary to Minister in Copenhagen, 18.8.1917.

96. Shub, p. 343.

97. Ludendorff, **My War Memories**, Vol II, pp. 509-10.

98. Golder, pp. 359-72.

99. Hoffmann, Vol II, pp. 178-85.

100. Brussilov, p. 315.

101. Hoffmann, Vol II, p. 185.

102 Wheeler-Bennett, p. 56.

103 Schulz, p. 260.

104 Wheeler-Bennett, p 6l.

105 Zeman, p. 242.

106. V I Lenin, **Select Works Vol II, Part I** (London, 1953) p. 333.

107. **Ibid., loc.cit.**

108. **Ibid.**, p. 331.

109. **Ibid.,** p. 178.

110. **Ibid.**, pp. 178-79.

111. Jane Degras, **Soviet Documents on Foreign Policy, Vol I** (London, 1951) p. 3-4.

112. Wheeler-Bennett, pp. 71-74.

113. Shub, p. 296.

114. Degras, p. 10.

115. Zeman, p. 246.

116. Zeman, **G R R**, pp 81-83, A38075, Counsellor of Legation in Stockholm to the Chancellor, 12.11.1917.

117. **Ibid., loc.cit.**

118. Kitchen. p. 107.

119. Schulz, p. 74.

120. Hoffmann, **My War Memories, Vol II**, p. 190.

121. Zeman **G R R**, pp. cellor, 10.11.1917.

122. **Ibid.**, p. 75, AS418l, State Secretary of the Foreign Ministry to State Secretary of the Treasury, 9.11.1917.

123 **Ibid.**, p. 93, AS4446, Under State Secretary to Minister in Bern.

124. **Ibid**, pp. 94-95, AS4486, State Secretary to the Foreign Ministry Liaison Officer at General Headquarters. 3.12.1917.

125. **Ibid.,** p. 96, AS4607, Liaison Officer at the Imperial Court to Foreign Ministry, 4.12.1917.

126. Degras, pp. 11-12.

127 Wheeler-Bennett, p.85.

128 **Ibid**. p.87.

129. **Ibid.**, p. 78

130. Zeman, p. 252

131. Degras, pp. 12-13

132. Hoffmann, Vol II, p. 191.

133. Ibid., p. 193.

134. Ibid., p. 194.

135. Ibid., p. 193.

136. Trotsky, p. 90.

137. Hoffmann, p. 194.

138. Ludendorff, My **War Memories, Vo.1 II**, p. 512.

139. **Ibid., loc.cit.**

140. Degras, pp. 18-21.

141. **Ibid., loc.cit.**

142. Ludendorff, **The General Staff Vol II**, pp 475-76.

143. **Ibid.**, pp. 491-98.

144. Hindenburg, p. 162.

145. Ludendorff, **The General Staff, Vol II**, pp. 379-80.

146. Ludendorff, **My War Memories, Vol II**, pp. 534-35

147. Wheeler-Bennett, pp. 107-11.

148. Degras, pp. 21-22.

149. Wheeler-Bennett, pp. 118-19.

150 Hoffmann, Vol II, p. 199.

151 Wheeler-Bennett, pp. 102-03.

152 Count Ottokar Czernin, **In the World War,** (London, 1919), p.250-51.

153. Hoffmann, Vol II, pp. 199-200.

154. **Ibid.**, p. 200.

155. Czernin, p. 224.

156. Hoffmann, Vol II, p. 201.

157. Ludendorff, **My War Memories Vol II**, p. 545.

158. **Ibid.**, p. 545.

159. **Ibid.**, p. 546.

160. **Ibid., loc.cit.**

161. Hoffmann, Vol II, p. 203.

162. Wheeler-Bennett, p. 125.

163. Czernin, p. 228

164. Kitchen. p. 163.

165. Hoffmann, Vol II, pp. 203-4.

166. **Ibid.**, p. 204.

167. Wheeler-Bennett, pp. 127-28.

168. **Ibid.**, p. 128.

169. **Ibid.**, pp. 129-30.

170 Kitchen, p. 164.

171 Hoffmann, Vol II., pp. 204-5.

172 **Ibid.**, p.205.

173. **Ibid.**, pp. 205-6.

174. Ludendorff, **My War Memories Vol II**, pp. 547-8

175. **Ibid.**, pp. 524-28.

176. Kitchen, p. 171.

177. Ludendorff, **My War Memories Vol II**, pp. 531-42.

178. Hoffmann Vol II, p. 207.

179. Degras, p. 25.

180. Shub, p. 331.

181. V I Lenin, **Select Works Vol II Part 1**, pp. 365-67.

182. **Ibid.**, pp. 365-66.

183. Degras, p. 26.

184. Kitchen, p. 175.

185. Wheeler-Bennett, pp. 156-57.

186. Hoffmann, Vol II, p.209.

187. Wheeler-Bennett, pp. 158-59.

188. Hoffmann, p. 209.

189. Ibid., pp. 211-12.

190. Czernin, p. 237.

191. Hoffmann, Vol II p. 209.

192. **Ibid.,** p. 213.

193. Czernin, pp. 240-41.

194. Wheeler-Bennett, p. 170.

195. **Ibid., loc.cit.**

196. Czernin, pp. 237-40.

197. Shub, p. 334.

198. Degras, pp. 34-39.

199. **Ibid., loc.cit.**

200. **Ibid., loc.cit.**

201. **Ibid., loc.cit.**

202. Wheeler-Bennett, p. 192.

203. **Ibid.,** pp. 192-93.

204. Ludendorff, **My War Memories Vol II**, p. 552.

205. Wheeler-Bennett, pp 199-200.

206. **Ibid.,** p. 207.

207. Hoffmann, Vol II p. 216.

208. **Ibid., loc.cit.**

209. **Ibid.,** pp. 216-17.

210. Czernin. pp. 241-45.

211. **Ibid.**, p. 245.

212. **Ibid.**, p. 247.

213. Ibid., **loc.cit.**

214. Ludendorff, **My War Memories Vol II**, p. 555

215. Hindenburg, p. 311.

216. Ludendorff, **My War Memories Vol II**, pp. 555-56.

217. Czernin, p.248.

218. **Ibid.**, p. 249.

219. Hoffmann, Vol II, p. 217.

220. Degras, pp. 41-43.

221. Ibid., **loc.cit.**

222. Hoffmann, Vol II pp. 218-19.

223. Trotsky, p. 143.

224. Ian Grey, **The First Fifty Years - Soviet Russia 1917-67** (London, 1967), p.128.

225. Hoffmann, Vol II, p. 219.

226. Hindenburg, p. 246.

227. Ludendorff, **My War Memories Vol II**, p. 557.

228. **Ibid.**, p. 559.

229. Ludendorff, **General Staff Vol II**, pp. 548-50.

230. Wheeler-Bennett, pp 231-32.

231. Kitchen, pp 179-80.

232. Zeman, pp. 274-75.

233. V I Lenin, **Select Works Vol II** Part 1, pp. 395-96.

234. Hoffmann, Vol II, p. 206.

235. Shub, pp. 337-38.

236. **Ibid.**, p. 338

237. Kitchen, p. 181.

238. Shub, p. 338.

239. Zeman, p. 278.

240. Degras, p. 46.

241. Hoffmann, Vol I, pp, 207-8.

242. **Ibid.**, p. 207.

243. Degras. pp. 48-50.

244 V I Lenin, **Select Works Vol II, Part 1**, pp. 397-406.

245 V I Lenin, **Select Works Vol II**, (Moscow, 1970), p. 573.

246 **Ibid., loc.cit.**

247. V I Lenin, **Select Works, Vol II, Part 1**, pp 409-10.

248. Hoffmann, Vol I, p. 208.

249. Kitchen, p. 181.

250. **Ibid.**, pp. 183-4.

251. Zeman **G R R** p. 119, ASl26l, State Secretary to Foreign Ministry, 11.3.1917.

252. Hoffmann, Vol II, pp. 221-23.

253. Czernin, p. 251.

254 **Ibid.**, p. 255.

255   Hindenburg, p.247.

256   Zeman **G R R,** p.128, A20991, Minister in Moscow to the Foreign Ministry, 17.5.1918.

257. **Ibid.,** pp. 128-9, A20991, State Secretary to Minister in Moscow, 18.5.1918.

258. **Ibid.,** pp. 120-21, A19757, Minister in Moscow to the Chancellor, 30.4.1918.

259   Shub, pp. 340-41.

260   Trotsky, p.143.

Chapter Three

The Armistice and Bolshevism

"Everything was destroyed, commercial treaties and treaties of alliance, conventions between State and State relating to the most jealously guarded interests, the public and private law of every state. The elite of the greater European nations, and more especially its youth who would have been called to govern in ten or fifteen years time, were mown down ... Everywhere the balance of wealth was upset ... The national fortune even of the richest peoples, was heavily mortgaged in order to meet gigantic war obligations"[1]

When the first Penary Session of the Peace Conference opened in Paris on 18th January 1919 the problems facing the statesmen of the victorious Entente Powers were not confined to the formulation of a peace agreement with the defeated Central Powers against the backcloth of a war weary and politically unstable Europe, but also encompassed the singular problem posed by the presence of a Bolshevik regime established in Moscow. That the political regime which came into being in the November Revolution in Russia in 1917 was a major consideration to those concerned with bringing order to the situation of social and political unrest existing throughout Europe is widely attested:

> *"The effect of the Russian problem on the Paris Conference ... was profound: Paris cannot be understood without Moscow. Without ever being represented at Paris at all, the Bolsheviki and Bolshevism were powerful elements at every turn. Russia played a more vital part at Paris than Prussia! For the Prussian idea had been utterly defeated, while the Russian idea was still rising in power."*[2]

> *"The peacemakers themselves attached considerable importance to the Russian operation. In preparing for the conference they placed Russian affairs high on its agenda. The Russian problem cropped up repeatedly during consultations among the Western Statemen before the opening of the conference. In the first two weeks of the conference the Allied rulers spent more time discussing Russia than any other subject, and they returned to it frequently during the remainder of the conference."*[3]

Yet even before the fighting of the First World War had been concluded Bolshevism had begun,

> *"... to play a role in shaping the pattern of the peace to follow."*[4]

and contributed to the debate within the nations of both belligerent camps as to the nature of the Armistice that was to come into being. The format that the

Armistice was to take was a subject of contention within the Entente, bringing into conflict the proponents of a negotiated peace and those who, after years of unparalleled human sacrifice and hardship, were determined upon securing an unconditional surrender. The touchstone for the debate can be held to be the German note to President Wilson of 3rd October 1918 which was delivered by the Swiss Ambassador to the United States to the Department of State in Washington on 7th October 1918. Addressed personally to President Wilson the note requested an immediate armistice and further asked the President to,

> "... take steps for the restoration of peace, to notify all belligerents of this request, and to invite them to delegate plenipotentiaries for the purpose of taking up negotiations. The German Government accepts, as the basis for its negotiations, the program laid down by the President of the United States ..."

The debate among the Entente Powers over the terms of an Armistice which the German note heralded was to owe as much to the vicissitudes of the domestic politics of the Allied nations as it did to any appreciation of the wider European situation. Indeed, the whole period of international debate from the early days of October 1918 until the conclusion of the Paris conference was to reveal the close interplay of domestic and foreign policy considerations.

Yet, as the German note made explicit, the basis upon which an armistice might first be brought into effect, and perhaps the foundation upon which a lasting peace could possibly be seen to be built, stemmed from a programme developed by President Wilson. This programme was first elaborated in President Wilson's address to the Joint Session of Congress on 8th January 1918 and became known as the "Fourteen Points". This speech was to provide the focus about which unity and disagreement were to vacillate both within and between the major powers in the hard bargaining of the months to come. Although the essence of President Wilson's speech is well known, such was its impact upon the Armistice negotiations and the deliberations of the Peace Conference which followed, it is worth recording its details:

I.   Open covenants of peace, openly arrived at, after which there shall be no private international understandings of any kind but diplomacy shall proceed always frankly and in the public view.

II.   Absolute freedom of navigation upon the seas, outside territorial waters, alike in peace and in war, except national action for the enforcement of international covenants.

III.   The removal, so far as possible, of all economic barriers and the establishment of an equality of trade conditions among all the nations consenting to the peace and associating themselves for its maintenance.

IV.   Adequate guarantees given and taken that national armaments will be reduced to the lowest point consistent with domestic safety.

V.   A free, open-minded, and absolutely impartial adjustment of all colonial claims, based upon a strict observance of the principle that in determining all such questions of sovereignty the interests of the populations concerned must have equal weight with the equitable claims of the government whose title is to be determined.

VI. The evacuation of all Russian territory and such a settlement of all questions affecting Russia as will secure the best and freest cooperation of the other nations of the world in obtaining for her an unhampered and unembarrassed opportunity for the independent determination of her own political development and national policy and assure her of a sincere welcome into the society of free nations under institutions of her own choosing; and, more than a welcome, assistance also of every kind that she may need and may herself desire. The treatment accorded Russia by her sister nations in the months to come will be the acid test of their good will, of their comprehension of her needs as distinguished from their own interests, and of their intelligent and unselfish sympathy.

VII. Belgium, the whole world will agree, must be evacuated and restored, without any attempt to limit the sovereignty which she enjoys in common with all other free nations. No other single act will serve as this will serve to restore confidence among the nations in the laws which they have themselves set and determined for the government of their relations with one another. Without this healing act the whole structure and validity of international law is forever impaired.

VIII. All French territory should be freed and the invaded portions restored, and the wrong done to

France by Prussia in 1871 in the matter of Alsace-Lorraine, which has unsettled the peace of the world for nearly fifty years, should be righted, in order that peace may once more be made secure in the interest of all.

IX. A readjustment of the frontiers of Italy should be effected along clearly recognisable lines of nationality.

X. The peoples of Austria-Hungary, whose place among the nations we wish to see safeguarded and assured, should be accorded the freest opportunity of autonomous development.

XI Rumania, Serbia, and Montenegro, should be evacuated; occupied territories restored; Serbia accorded free and secure access to the sea; and the relations of the several Balkan states to one another determined by friendly counsel along historically established lines of allegiance and nationality; and international guarantees of the political and economic independence and territorial integrity of the several Balkan states should be entered into.

XII. The Turkish portions of the present Ottoman Empire should be assured a secure sovereignty, but the other nationalities which are now under Turkish rule should be assured an undoubted security of life and an absolutely unmolested opportunity of autonomous development, and the Dardonelles should be permanently opened as a free passage to the ships and commerce of all nations under international guarantees.

XIII. An independent Polish state should be erected which should include the territories inhabited by indisputably Polish populations, which should be assured a free and secure access to the sea, and whose political and economic independence and territorial integrity should be guaranteed by international covenant.

XIV. A general association of nations must be formed under specific covenants for the purpose of affording mutual guarantees of political independence and territorial integrity to great and small states alike.

The German request for negotiations leading to an armistice was without doubt reached after an assessment of the capability and capacity of her armed forces to attain military victory in the war, and an assessment of the domestic political climate. These two analytically separate considerations were in fact simply different facets of the same problem, namely, could Germany expect to secure the defeat of the Entente, and if not, what was to become of the post-war Germany? With the impossibility of a military victory being achieved by the Central Powers the answer to the second part of the question was to a large extent dependent upon the nature of the armistice which could be negotiated.

Although 1916 had appeared to the Entente as the year in which military victory would be attained over the Central Powers the failure of the offensives on the Western Front during the summer of that year testified to the fact that victory lay far in the future. Field Marshall Kitchener's New Armies had sustained terrible losses in the offensive along the River Somme and the French were still engaged in an Herculean struggle at Verdun which so sapped their strength and coloured the thinking of her military commanders that they were never to recapture their earlier offensive zest. Yet the Germans did not consider 1916 to have been a year of military success for their cause, despite having held the offensives launched against them on the Western Front. Into their assessment the Germans had to take cognizance of the Russian offensive in Galicia which had broken through the Austrian Front, nor could they ignore the entry of Rumania into the war against them bringing as it did 750,000 fresh troops into the opposing front line. After the initial successes of 1914 and 1915 the Central Powers found that 1916 was the year in which they had been forced back on to the defensive; the speed and successes of their earlier advances had become a thing of the past and although in the West they had yielded none of the ground they had earlier gained the prospects of making further inroads into French territory seemed remote. Erich von Falkenhayn as Chief of the German General Staff seemed to be no longer capable of securing the German victory which had appeared to be such a real and attractive possibility in the early days of the hostilities. His planning of the February offensive in which he had envisaged the destruction of the French Army by the attack upon Verdun had not brought the anticipated results, for whilst tremendously heavy losses had been inflicted upon the French, German losses paralleled them with disheartening symmetry and the fortresses of Verdun were still not relinquished by their defenders.[5] On the River Somme the British attacks were held and although the German defenders were inflicting heavier losses on the attackers than they themselves were sustaining the ultimate difference was not great and the gradual erosion of the German defensive line was doing little to strengthen the morale of the German forces. Von Falkenhayn's failure to secure further swift and decisive victories led to pressure upon the Kaiser to remove him from his post and Falkenhayn resigned on 28th August 1916 to be replaced by Field Marshal Paul von Hindenburg and his Chief of Staff General von Ludendorff; men who had recorded a string of victories over the Russian forces on the Eastern Front starting with the breaking of the Russian advances at the battles of Tannenberg and the Masurian Lakes and followed by a series of counter attacks which had driven the Russian Army well back on to its own soil.[6]

With the change in the military command came a change in the conduct of the war effort. Ludendorff, in particular, was a firm advocate of conducting a "total' war", of harnessing all of Germany's resources to the attainment of military victory. For Ludendorff, peace could not be attained by diplomatic means but only by force of arms and the defeat of the military forces ranged against the Central Powers. The peace which Ludendorff envisaged military success producing, the "Hindenburg Peace", was to entail the imposition of treaties upon the defeated nations of the Entente Powers; a victorious Germany was to annex large areas of Russian and French territory and to incorporate Belgium into the German Empire, only in this way argued Ludendorff, could Germany be assured of her preparedness for any future European conflict.[7] To this end, Hindenburg and Ludendorff became increasingly involved in German domestic politics arguing that the German politicians were acting in a manner destructive to the attainment of military victory. In particular, they despised the delay occasioned by the political manoeuvrings of the Imperial Chancellor, von Bethmann-Hollweg, in seeking the opinion and approval of all shades of political opinion represented in the Reichstag as to the conduct of the war.

Two issues especially highlighted their frustration with the politicians in general and Bethmann-Hollweg in particular; the delay which this consultative process caused to the universal war service bill which they had demanded and which would have resulted in all German males between the ages of sixteen and sixty not already in uniform being drafted into auxiliary service under the direction of the Ministry of War, and secondly, the reluctance of the Foreign Office to support the re-introduction of unrestricted submarine warfare for fear of bringing the United States into the war; a fear to which Bethmann-Hollweg was a subscriber.[8] To end the delay occasioned by the political process and Bethmann-Hollweg's adherence to consultation, Hindenburg and Ludendorff approached the Kaiser directly and implied that unless unrestricted submarine warfare became operative by 1st February 1917 they would not be either in a position to, nor prepared to, offer any guarantees as to the outcome of the war.[9]

In pursuing this line of argument Hindenburg and Ludendorff discounted the opposing arguments that Germany did not have the submarine capacity to destroy British merchant shipping and that the inevitable entry of the United States into the war could ensure an Entente victory. Instead they vigorously maintained that Britain would be deprived of vital food and war supplies and would be forced out of the war and that German control of the seas would make it impossible for United States' troops to be deployed on the Western Front. [10] In these arguments they were successful. The Spring of 1917 boded well for the Central Powers. General Nivelle's offensive on the Rive Aisne had been held and with it the offensive role of the French Army had irretrievably become a thing of the past, the effects of the war were now clearly being felt by the French forces and in consequence morale suffered as manifested in a series of mutinies, [11] and in Russia the Czar had been deposed and the fighting capacity of the Russian forces was very much open to question in the wake of the February Revolution.[12] Yet despite these encouraging signs the military situation in the summer of 1917 was far from favourable from the German viewpoint. The Entente blockade was reaching its height, military victories were in short supply, the submarine campaign upon which such high hopes had been placed had fallen short of producing the results anticipated for supplies of food and war materials were still reaching Britain from across the Atlantic Ocean in such quantities as to suggest that Britain was unlikely to be starved out of the war and, perhaps most discouraging of all, the United States had entered the war on the side of the Entente although no American troops had taken up position in the front line.

By forcing the resignation of Bethmann-Hollweg on 12th July 1917 by threat of their resignation and securing the appointment of Dr Georg Michaelis as Imperial Chancellor, Hindenburg and Ludendorff increased their control over all aspects of the war effort.[13] The failure of an attempt by the Reichstag to force Michaelis and the Supreme Command to seek a negotiated peace ensured that Hindenburg and Ludendorff could now operate virtually as they chose free of constraints from the civilian government.[14]

In the beginning the control of the Supreme Command over the war effort produced positive results for the German cause. Ludendorff successfully accomplished the return of Lenin to Russia, a factor calculated to further weaken a member of the Entente camp already incapacitated by a lack of military success and the absence of any clearly **discernible** centre of political authority within. In a matter of weeks the value of this initiative produced the best possible result for the German efforts with a now Bolshevik Russia suing for peace and by doing so offering Germany the opportunity not only of transferring troops from the Eastern to the Western Front but also of making use of Russian resources of food and war, materials. The German economy was placed under the control of General Wilhelm Groener [15], whilst on the Western Front, Ludendorff opted to maintain the defensive posture of the German forces throughout the winter of 1917-18 in the face of huge British offensives; a tactic which worked very much in favour of the defenders, as attested by the losses sustained by the attackers at Passchendaele.[16] To these favourable omens for the Central Powers must be added the victory secured by the Austrians over the Italians at the battle of Caporetto in October 1917 which necessitated British and French troops being sent to the aid of their Italian ally.[17] Yet, with the coming of 1918 even these successes were not without qualification.

At the strategic level the reasoning which had in past led to the resignation of Bethmann-Hollweg had been shown to be faulty. The unrestricted submarine warfare so vociferously demanded by the Supreme Command had not brought Britain to the point of starvation and capitulation as had been envisaged, also it had led to United States involvement in the war and United State troops were entering Europe on a growing scale. Additionally, the benefits hoped for from the November Revolution in Russia had not been of the magnitude anticipated; the Brest-Litovsk negotiations were proving to be a long drawn out affair and the call for international peace and the overthrow of the belligerent governments by their own working classes emanating from Moscow coupled with a plea for international peace were receiving a far from hostile reception among the German people and certain sections of the armed forces.[18] At the same time many in Germany were proving as receptive to a negotiated peace based on the Fourteen Points of President Wilson as were those in the Entente camp.[19] Peace, for many in Germany, had replaced the hopes and thoughts of military victory which they had hitherto entertained. Discontent with the war among the German population was undoubtedly exacerbated by food shortages; the Germans and not the British were being starved out of the war. After the Kohlsuben winter of 1916-17, the winter of 1917-18 proved even more severe and food shortages were a major factor in the strike of 400,000 Berlin munitions workers at the end of January 1918 which was only put down by the use of troops and threats of front line military service for the more active participants in the strike. [20]

These events served to convince Ludendorff that the German forces had to abandon their previously held defensive posture on the Western Front and seek victory before the arrival of yet more American troops in Europe made such an objective an impossibility. On this basis the "Ludendorff Offensive" was launched on the Western Front in the Spring of 1918. Utilising troops released from the Eastern Front by Russia's withdrawal from the war, Ludendorff's plan was to drive a wedge between the British and French armies and to reach the Channel ports. In the early stages this audacious plan looked capable of being fulfilled as the allied front was pushed back to the River Marne the scene of heavy fighting in the opening months of the war.[21] The initial successes, however, could not be sustained, and by June the German advance had been held and General Foch was in a position to counter attack with superior troops and equipment.

The armies of the Entente were now markedly stronger than their German opponents and in the early days of August the Australian Army Corps breached the German lines and was only stopped by ferocious and costly resistance.[22] Under this onslaught the morale of the German troops began to waver for this was not the German army of the first two years of war but an army which had in its ranks those who had been exposed to Bolshevik propaganda on the Eastern Front, and some of those who had been in the forefront of the January strikes in Berlin.[23] It was an army poorly provisioned and subjected to the clandestine propaganda of the Spartacus Letters calling for revolt at home and peace abroad.[24]

Even so, in July 1918 the Supreme Command was unwilling to concede that military victory lay beyond the compass of the German forces, yet by August doubts had emerged,

> *"In July the Secretary of State for Foreign Affairs, Paul von Hintze, asked Ludendorff bluntly whether he was 'certain of finally and decisively beating the enemy.' 'I can reply to that with a decided yes' was Ludendorff's answer ... A month later the furthest that Ludendorff would go was to admit that the German Army was no longer capable of a 'great offensive' although he claimed that by a skilful defensive policy he could break the Allies' morale so that they would sue for peace."[25]*

September 1918 saw the ending of any hope of a break in Allied morale. American attacks between the Argonne and the Meuse followed by a French attack west of the Argonne and supported by British and Belgium offensives heralded the beginning of the end for the German forces on the Western Front.[26] On 29th September, Germany's ally Bulgaria sued for peace and in doing so exposed the Central Powers' southern flank. No longer could hopes of a military victory for Germany or hopes of the Entente suing for peace be entertained. On the same day Ludendorff announced to the Kaiser, the Imperial Chancellor and the Foreign Secretary that the war was lost, that armistice must be immediately sought and that to facilitate this, a liberalisation of the German Government be undertaken. [27]

Two days after the dismissal of Ludendorff for fear that his retention in office would jeopardise the negotiations with President Wilson that Ludendorff's own insistence had produced the newly appointed Imperial Chancellor, Prince Max von Baden, introduced a series of important constitutional changes which were passed by the Reichstag and Bundesrat on 28th October 1918. These reforms served two purposes. Firstly, they undoubtedly owed their initiation to President Wilson's intimation that he would not negotiate with a German government which he could see as being essentially similar to its predecessors; so some form of democratisation was obligatory if an armistice sponsored by President Wilson and conforming to his Fourteen Points was to be arrived at. Secondly, they satisfied the political demands which since the 1880's had been voiced by the Centre, the Progressives and the Social Democratic parties in German politics. In essence, the reforms,

> "... promised effective parliamentary government with a real measure of ministerial responsibility; and most important in the present context, they subordinated the military and naval commands to the civilian government."[28]

Yet these reforms, which promised so much, were never really implemented for within a week of their notification Germany was enveloped in domestic turmoil. The Kiel naval mutiny and the refusal of the Kaiser to abdicate were the starting points for civil disorder throughout Germany. Kurt Eisner, the leader of the Independent Socialists, was not convinced that the reforms went far enough in achieving a clear departure from the past, a break he saw as necessary if Germany were to secure a "just peace", and he established a soldiers' and workers' council in Munich and proclaimed the Bavarian Republic on 7th November. This example was quickly followed in Cologne, Frankfurt, Leipzig and Stuttgart. In the face of this clear hostility Prince Max surrendered office to the Majority Socialists and on 9th November, Scheidemann proclaimed the establishment of the German Republic. Friedrich Ebert assumed the role of Chancellor. It was at this juncture that political necessity and a shared fear of Bolshevism gaining a grip upon a Germany verging on revolution forced the army and the civilian government to reach an agreement of mutual benefit but which itself was,

> "... destined to save both parties from the extreme
> elements of revolution but, as a result of which, the
> Weimer Republic was doomed at birth."[29]

General Wilhelm Groener, who replaced Ludendorff as Quartermaster-General upon the dismissal of the latter, was in receipt of the terms of the Armistice which had been communicated to him by the Entente Powers and needed a civilian government capable of assuming the responsibility for their acceptance. In addition, Groener needed the army to have a legitimate government to which to owe its allegiance for with the abdication of the Kaiser it was only by serving such a government that the office corps would have the opportunity of maintaining control over its troops who otherwise could switch their allegiance to the soldiers councils which were appearing in ever increasing numbers:

> "These considerations led (Groener) on the night of
> 9th November to make his now famous telephone call

*to Friedrich Ebert, the leader of the Majority
Socialists and the new Chancellor of the Reich. In the
course of the brief conversation, he promised that the
present High Command would continue its
functions until the troops had been brought back to
Germany in good order and perfect discipline. This
was, at least implicitly, an admission that the army
recognised the legitimacy of the new regime, but it
was, nevertheless, a conditional recognition. Groener
made it clear that the officer corps expected the
government to aid it in maintaining discipline in the
army, in securing the army's sources of supply, and
in preventing the disruptions of the railway system
during the army's march home."[30]*

Perhaps of greatest significance, however, was the
consensus between Groener, the soldier, and Ebert, the
politician, upon the internal enemy that Germany was
now facing, Bolshevism. For the alliance between
Groener and Ebert, between the army and the
government, owed much to the threat that Bolshevism
was seen as presenting to Germany:

*"... (Groener) stressed the fact that the officer corps
looked to the government to combat Bolshevism and
was putting itself at the governments disposal
primarily for that purpose"* [31]

Like Prince Max von Baden before him, Ebert had
been obliged to fight on two fronts at the same time;
against chaos and the ever present threat of revolution
at home, and against a punitive peace enforced from
abroad.[32] Domestic and foreign policy were inseparable.
To resolve the problems at home, the government was
obliged to provide food and employment and some

measure of assurance of a "just peace". In turn, the provision of food, employment and peace were dependent upon the actions which the victorious Entente took toward the defeated Germany. As Mayer notes:

"On the one hand, the Allies were not likely to assist a weak government which in order to survive might decree economic and social reforms that the Allies considered too advanced; on the other hand, there would be little., if any, inducement to the victors to grant a Wilsonian peace should this government succeed in restoring and maintaining order by sheer repression."[33]

Both Prince Max and Ebert drew the correct conclusion in assuming that the Entente were not in favour of the development of Bolshevism in Germany or of the German making some agreement of mutual advantage with the Bolsheviks. Therefore, the threat of a Bolshevik Germany seemed a possible theme which could be developed to Germany's advantage in dealing with the Entente over the question of an armistice. If the threat of a Bolshevik Germany was to be the lever employed in the Armistice negotiations, the question still to be considered was the amount of weight to be placed upon it for the maximum effect to result:

"should (the leaders of the new German Republic) exaggerate the strength of the Spartacists, the extent of Soviet supported subversion, the shortage of food and unemployment? How terrifying could they make the Bolshevik spectre without risking a loss of credibility? Should they renew diplomatic relations with Soviet Russia? Alternatively, should the

German government offer to join the Allies in their containment of and intervention in Bolshevik Russia?"[34]

Although no firm line of action could be said to have emerged from these questions and "muddling through" became the order of the day, there is little doubt but that the Germans did make constant use of the threat of Bolshevism. Certainly the German representatives at the Armistice negotiations used the threat of a Bolshevik Germany throughout the various stages of debate. Under the leadership of Matthias Erzberger the German delegation deliberately employed the spectre of Bolshevism, contending that excessively severe Armistice conditions would give rise to the development of Bolshevism in Germany.[35] They even went so far as to argue that should Bolshevism gain a hold upon Germany then the Entente Powers would themselves be imperilled, not simply because of the contagious nature of the "disease" but because of the inability of a Bolshevik Germany to pay any reparations which might be imposed upon her. They maintained that Germany could become the bulwark against Bolshevism which the Entente could remove only by risk to themselves. The "Bolshevik horror" was utilised by the German delegation on various specific points of the Armistice provisions such as the evacuation of the left bank of the Rhine, setting a time limit for evacuation from occupied territories, reducing the weapons of the German forces, and the continuation of the Entente blockade.[36] Yet although these arguments met with but limited success, on one important clause of the Armistice relating to Soviet Russia the German reasoning did make the victors qualify their policy and that was in connection with Article XII which was concerned with the evacuation of German troops from Soviet territory:

"All German troops at present on any territory which before the war formed part of Austria-Hungary, Rumania, or Turkey, shall withdraw within the frontiers of Germany as they existed on August 1, 1914, and all German troops at present in territories which before the war formed part of Russia, must likewise return to within the frontiers of Germany, as above defined, as soon as the Allies shall think the moment suitable, having regard to the internal situation of these territories"[37]

The fact that the German evacuation of Russian territory was not to be immediate but at a time to be designated by the victors was in conflict with the sixth of President Wilson's Fourteen Points which had demanded the evacuation of all Russian territory, and at a meeting on 5th October 1918 the Prime Ministers of Britain, France and Italy had themselves agreed upon a recommendation calling for the German evacuation of the Caucasus and all the territory of pre-war Russia. Article XII marks a clear break with that line of thought, a break which can be attributed to a growing realisation on the part of the victors powers that a withdrawal of German forces from the Russian territory which they had occupied during the course of the war would create a power vacuum into which the Bolsheviks would move. The idea of using German troops as a temporary barrier to Bolshevism gained increased support within the Entente as the Armistice approached:

"In early 1918 some of the British government, such as Lord Milner, secretary of war at the time, were talking of the possibility of a negotiated peace in which 'the gains of Germany on Russian soil' would compensate her for colonial and other losses. On the eve of the Armistice, Lord Milner and General Sir Henry Wilson told Colonel House that they were disposed to object to German demobilisation on the grounds that Germany might have to serve as a bulwark against Bolshevism."[38]

If the victors feared the westward spread of Bolshevism they were also possessed of another fear which went some way to counter-balancing it, namely, that of the possibility of an agreement being reached between Germany and the new Soviet state and especially of German economic domination of Soviet Russia in the post-war period.[39]

With the approach of the Armistice the Entente was undecided about the future of German troops on Russian soil. On the one hand those troops represented a possible means of limiting the westward spread of Bolshevism, yet on the other they could be viewed as the means by which Germany could utilise her hold on Russia for her own ends. Certainly they were well aware of the dilemma which the existence of those troops presented to the Entente and on 9th November 1918, the day after the opening of the Armistice negotiations, the German delegation protested at the immediate withdrawal of their troops from Russian territory on the grounds that Bolshevism would triumph in the wake of their evacuation. On 10th November the compromise solution on the German forces in Soviet Russia was reached and included in Article XII.

If Article XII of the Armistice was the single most important element relating to Russia, Articles XXV and XXIX were not without significance, requiring as they did the Germans to open the Black Sea and the Baltic Sea to the Entente Powers:

> "This provided the Allies with relatively direct and easy access to European Russia and to areas controlled or endangered by Bolshevism. Further intervention, for which British and French leaders were then pressing, could be carried out via the western and southern sea approaches to Russia with far greater facility than by the roundabout routes which the North Russian and Siberian expeditions of the summer of 1918 had had to utilise. The French sponsored expedition to Odessa in December 1918 took advantage of the Black Sea route. In addition, supplies could now be shipped directly to anti-Bolshevik forces in South Russia and the Baltic area." [40]

Finally, Article XV of the Armistice required the Germans to renounce the Treaty of Brest-Litovsk and Article XXIX obligated them to surrender to the Entente the Russian Black Sea and merchant fleets which they had acquired in 1918. Article XIX required the Germans to release into the trust of the Entente, prior to their eventual return to Russia, the gold reserves which Germany had received from the Soviet government under the Treaty of Brest-Litovsk. At the Armistice negotiations Bolshevism was both a military and political problem to the Entente, just as it had been when the Soviet government sued for peace with the Central Powers immediately upon assuming office after the November Revolution of 1917. The only change which had arisen from the viewpoint of the Entente was that with the defeat of the Central Powers, Bolshevism was now a factor with which they were forced to deal and resolve.

In playing the "Bolshevik Card" at the Armistice negotiations the German delegation was in part responding to the reality of political life in Germany at the time and in part playing upon the undoubted anxiety which Bolshevism engendered in the minds of the statesmen of the Entente Powers. Whether, with hindsight, it can be held that the threat of Bolshevism at home and abroad was exaggerated in the minds of the politicians of the victor powers is not of great importance. What is of significance is the perceptions which they entertained of the nature of the threat which they saw Bolshevism containing, for it was these perceptions which influenced their decisions about the need to bring to a speedy conclusion the hostilities of the First World War and the form which the peace that was to follow was to take.

Even before the Armistice had been signed, the problem that Bolshevism posed for the states of Europe had been occasioning apprehension and anxiety among the statesmen of the Entente. On 30th October 1918, Lloyd-George and Clemenceau at a meeting with Colonel House had considered the danger inherent in Bolshevism, and Lloyd-George had gone so far as to admit that,

"... it was possible to create such a state of affairs (the appearance of Bolshevism) in England, and both

(Lloyd-George and Clemenceau) agreed anything might happen in Italy."[41]

Likewise, President Wilson was far from convinced that the United States was immune to the appeal of Bolshevism:

"Although there was certainly no imminent danger of a Bolshevik revolution in America, even Wilson was troubled by what he interpreted as signs of future difficulty. On October 16, 1918, he told Sir William Wiseman, a confidential British representative in the United States: 'the spirit of Bolshevism is lurking everywhere... There is grave unrest all over the world. There are symptoms of it in this country - symptoms that are apparent although not yet dangerous'"[42]

Although watchful for signs of the appearance of Bolshevism in their own nations, the statesmen of the Entente were keenly aware that the states most likely to initially succumb were those of the defeated powers; Germany and Austria-Hungary.

This perception of the defeated states as fertile ground in which the seed of Bolshevism could flourish meant that the treatment of the vanquished by the victors had to be carefully considered. For some, Bolshevism was dependent for its success upon starvation and unemployment; if the emergence of these two evils could be prevented, or their presence eradicated, Bolshevism could be contained. In consequence, the victors would have to adopt a coupe of action in relation to their former opponents of providing food and economic assistance. Such a line of reasoning found favour with President Wilson:

*"In his address to Congress on the occasion of the
Armistice, President Wilson declared that relief for
the peoples of Europe will set their minds and
energies free for the great and hazardous task of
political reconstruction... Hunger does not breed
reform; it breeds madness and all the ugly distempers
that make an orderly life impossible."*[43]

and did not lack its advocates in Britain. But in France
such thinking did not gain the ascendency; in French
eyes the provision of food and especially economic
assistance to Germany was viewed as simply
encouraging the rebuilding of German power, whilst
the withholding of such assistance could be used as a
threat with which to pressure Germany over the terms
of the peace.

Yet the provision of food and economic assistance
was but one possible solution in the fight against
Bolshevism. The attempt to restrict the westward spread
of Bolshevism by the terms of the Armistice has
previously been referred to, and already the Entente had
been engaged in military intervention in Soviet Russia if
under the guise of maintaining an Eastern Front against
the Central Powers. Furthermore, President Wilson was
of the conviction that these measures of themselves
were only partial answers to the question which
Bolshevism presented to the non-Soviet world for
Bolshevism grew strongly wherever there was
dissatisfaction with the old political order and, in
consequence, Wilson held to the view that the
attainment of peace was not of itself sufficient to satisfy
the demands of the dissatisfied. Such satisfaction could
only be brought about by a just peace which met the
expectations of the people of the war-weary states; in

short, a peace which could not be brought about through coercion but a peace freely arrived at on the basis of President Wilson's Fourteen Points.

Yet in reality in November 1918 the Entente had a wide range of policies open to it in its dealings with the Soviet regime which had come to power in Russia. Thompson offers a most fitting summation of these possible policy alternatives,

> "At one extreme, the Allies, predicating their action on the threat by Bolshevism to Europe and the world, could intervene in Russia with their own troops, overwhelm the Soviet regime, and forcibly establish some type of "representative" government. At the other, they could withdraw their forces already in Russia, cut off aid to the anti-Bolsheviks, and let the Russians fight it out among themselves; if, as seemed likely Bolshevism should triumph, the Allies could attempt to blunt its expansionist drive and to win Soviet acquiescence in their plans for the postwar world by offering the Bolsheviks relief, economic aid, and trade. Between these extremes were a number of variants of the two positions: indirect intervention through moral and. material aid to the anti-Bolshevik forces in and around Russia; the isolation of Russia and the erection of a surrounding ring of buffer states to contain Bolshevism - a cordon sanitaire; mediation in an attempt to bring about a negotiated settlement of Russia's internal strife, which, in turn, might lead to her political self-determination under fair and peaceful conditions".[44]

Yet one course of action had already been embarked upon before the Armistice negotiations had commenced, namely, Allied intervention in Russia in the summer of 1918 and, in consequence of this, the freedom to successfully implement some of the policy alternatives mentioned by Thompson was severely curtailed and Allied policy toward Russia was to take on the appearance of "muddling through" as one policy was replaced, on occasions, by a policy which was almost its opposite, as policy alternatives were amalgamated only later to be separated.

The threat of Bolshevism was thus a problem to all of the parties to the Armistice negotiations. To the victorious Entente it represented a threat which the cessation of hostilities meant that they could not fail to attempt to resolve except at their own peril, and it conditioned the nature of the peace which they had to make with the vanquished. To the vanquished Bolshevism presented a pertinent domestic threat and a lever by which to exert pressure upon the victors in an effort to obtain a form of peace favourable to themselves. To both victors and vanquished alike, Bolshevism represented a new factor in the international politics of the post-war world with which they had to come to terms. For all of these reasons, Bolshevism and the new Soviet regime in Russia were important elements in the discussions which took place at the Armistice negotiations and were to be of still greater significance in the discussions at the Paris Peace Conference in 1919. In short, the ending of the war and the changing of the status-quo in Europe and the emergence of a Bolshevik regime in Russia changed the nature of the old pre-war international political order and were to shape the form that international relations was to assume in the new post-war international political system.

References

1.   Ferrero, Guglielmo. "Problems of Peace: From the Holy Alliance to the League of Nations" G P Putman, New York, 1919, p 260.

Lipson, E. "Europe 1914-1939" Adam and Charles Black, London 1957 has this to say about the cost of the First World War:

"The cost of the war of 1914-18 was commensurate with the scale of its operations; and an appalling price was exacted from victors and vanquished alike. Those who laid down their lives reached the staggering total of 8 millions, while the wounded amounted to 20 millions; and to these casualties in the field must be added the victims who succumbed to their hardships in the territories occupied or blockaded by the enemy. The expenditure lavished on the war attained astronomical proportions. Great Britain spent a daily average of 1 ½ million pounds down to March 1915, nearly 4 millions in 1915-16, 5 ½ millions in 1916-17, 6 ½ millions in 1917-18; and her national debt rose from 708 million pounds to 7,435 millions. The United States, who entered the war in 1917, raised in loans by the end of 1918 about 16,000 million dollars; the French national debt increased from 34,188 million francs to 147,472 millions; the German national debt mounted from 5,000 million marks to 160,000 millions." pp 307-308.

2. Baker, Ray Stannard. "Woodrow Wilson and World Settlement" William Heinemann Ltd. London, 1923, Vol II p64.

3. Thompson, John M. "Russia, Bolshevism, and the Versailles Peace" Princeton University Press, Princeton, NJ, 1966, p 4.

4. ibid p20.

5. Verdun remains, however, the only battle on the Western Front in the First World War in which the defenders sustained greater casualties than the attacking forces. For an illuminating account of this very significant battle see, Horne, Alistair. "Verdun : The Price of Glory" Macmillan, London, 1962.

6. Although nominally the subordinate member of the duo there' seems to be little to indicate that Ludendorff acted as such; indeed the weight of the evidence implies that his was the dominant influence upon the conduct of the war.

7. Watt, Richard M. "The King's Depart" The Literary Guild, London, 1969. p138.

8. An interesting account of the relationship between the Supreme Command and Chancellor Bethmann-Hollweg is to be found in Craig, Gordon A. "The Politics of the German Army 1640-1945" Oxford University Press, Oxford 1964. pp 313-326.

9. Watt op cit p136.

10. ibid.

11. Sumler, David. "A History of Europe in the 20th Century" The Dorsey Press, Homewood Ill. 1973 p50.

12. Silverlight, John. "The Victors Dilemma" Barrie and Jenkins Ltd, London, 1970, p5.

13. Dr Georg Michaelis held the post of Imperial Chancellor for but a few months to be replaced by Count Georg von Hertling. Both men were very much under the control of Hindenburg and Ludendorff. With the war effectively lost, Count von Hertling resigned on 3rd October 1918 to be replaced by Prince Max von Baden.

14. War weariness in Germany occasioned several deputies in the Reichstag to form a committee to draft a formal Peace Resolution. On July 19th, 1917, Matthias Erzberger introduced a resolution for peace that was passed by 212 votes to 126. The resolution was not, however, without reservation as the last paragraph reveals:

"As on August 1, 1914, so also now on the verge of a fourth year of war, the words of the speech from the Throne still hold: 'We are not impelled by the lust of conquest.' Germany took up arms in defence of her freedom, her independence, and the integrity of her soil.

The Reichstag strives for a peace of understanding and a lasting reconciliation of peoples. Any violations of territory, and political, economic, and financial persecutions are incompatible with such a peace. The Reichstag rejects any plan which proposes the imposition of economic barriers or the solidification of national hatreds after the war. The freedom of the seas must be maintained. Economic peace alone will lead to the friendly association of peoples. The Reichstag will promote actively the creation of international organisations of justice.

However, as long as the enemy governments refuse to agree to such a peace, as long as they threaten Germany and her allies with conquest and domination, so long will the German people stand united and unshaken, and they will fight until their right and that of their allies are made secure. Thus united, the German people remain unconquerable. The Reichstag feels that in this sentiment it is united with the men who have fought with courage to protect the Fatherland. The undying gratitude of our people goes out to them."

Cited in Snyder, Louis L. "Historical Documents of World War I" Van Nostrand. Princeton. NJ. 1958. p158.

15. Groener was later to mastermind the withdrawal of the German forces from the Western Front, and to a large extent it was the successful and orderly completion of this exercise which gave birth to the idea that the German army had not been defeated in battle but had been "stabbed in the back" by the politicians. The falsity of such a view is revealed by a note from Field Marshal Hindenburg to Prince von Baden dated 3rd October 1918:

"The Supreme Command insists on its demand of Sunday, 29th September, that a peace offer to our enemies be issued at once.

As a result of the collapse of the Macedonian Front and the weakening of our Western reserves which this has brought about, and now that it is impossible to make good the very considerable losses which have been incurred in the battles of the last few days, there is, so far as can be foreseen, no longer a prospect of forcing peace on the enemy.

The enemy, on the other hand, is continually bringing new and fresh reserves into the battle.

The German army still stands firm and successfully wards off all attacks. But the situation becomes daily more critical and may force the Supreme Command to take momentous decisions

It is desirable in the circumstances to break off the battle in order to spare the German people and its allies useless sacrifices. Every day wasted costs thousands of brave soldiers their lives."

Cited in von Baden Prince Max. "The Memoirs of Prince Max of Baden" Constable & Co Ltd. London 1928, vol II, p19.

16.   Hart, B H. Liddell, "History of the First World War" Book Club Associates. London, 1973, pp 423-434.

17.   ibid pp 449-456.

18. Wheeler-Bennett, J W. "Brest-Litovsk. The Forgotten Peace" Macmillan & Co Ltd. London 1963.

19. Watt. op cit p 141.

20. See the discussion which took place in the German War Cabinet at its meeting on 17th October 1918. Reported in Baden, Prince Max von. "The Memoirs of Prince Max of Baden" Constable & Co. Ltd. London 1928. Vol II, Ch V esp p 114.

21. Details of the battles of the "Ludendorff Offensive" are to be found in Hart, op cit. Ch VIII.

22. ibid. pp 541-551.

23. Watt op cit. p 143.

24. ibid.

25. ibid. pp 143-144.

26. Hart. op cit. pp 577-585.

27. Watt op cit. p 144.

28. Craig, op cit. pp 333-334.

29. Wheeler-Bennett, J W. "The Nemesis of Power: The German Army in Politics 1918-1945" Macmillan, London 1967. p 21.

30. Craig. op cit. p 348.

31. ibid. Authors' emphasis. Slightly different versions of this telephone conversation between Ebert and Groener appear in Wheeler—Bennett, J W. "Hindenburg: The Wooden Titan" Macmillan. London 1967. pp 207—208 and also in Carsten, F L. "The Reichswehr and Politics 1918-1933"

Oxford University Press, Oxford 1966. p 11. All three accounts, however, agree that an alliance between the civilian government and the army was necessary if the threat of a Bolshevik Germany was to be prevented.

32. Mayer, Arno J. "Politics and Diplomacy and Peacemaking" Weidenfeld and Nicolson, London 1968. p 92.

33. ibid.

34. ibid.

35. ibid p 93.

36. Thompson. op cit. p 23.

37. Rudin, Harry R. "Armistice 1918" Archon Books Hamden Conn. 1967. pp 428-429.

38. Thompson, op cit. p 25.

39. For a more detailed discussion of these fears see ibid pp 27-28.

40. ibid p 24.

41. ibid p 14.

42. cited ibid.

43. ibid. p 16.

44. ibid. p 38.

Chapter Four

Prelude to Rapallo: Germany and Russia at Paris

The context in which the armistice negotiations and the Paris Peace Conference were to take place was, to a large extent, circumscribed by a programme developed by Wilson:

> *"This programme was first elaborated in President Wilson's address to the Joint Session of Congress on 8th January 1918 and became known as the 'Fourteen Points'. This speech was to provide the focus about which unity and disagreement were to vacillate both within and between the major powers in the hard bargaining of the months to come."* [1]

The acceptance by the allies of the United States as well as by her German opponents of President Wilson's Fourteen Points probably owes as much, if not more, to the assessment which those nations made of the military situation with which they were confronted as it does to any intrinsic appeal which the President's programme possessed, or to his resolve in having that programme accepted as a basis for the conclusion of hostilities and the attainment of a lasting peace.

Despite having held the "Ludendorff Offensive" of March 1918 which had been intended to drive a wedge between the British and French armies on the Western Front and force the British back to the Channel ports, there were few signs in the Allied camp that they believed themselves to be in a position to secure a military victory over the Central Powers in 1918. Indeed, on 2nd June 1918 the Premiers of Britain, France and Italy, meeting at Versailles, had taken such a pessimistic view of the military situation facing them that they felt it necessary to call for immediate additional military support from the United States to stave off the threat of defeat:

> "We desire to express our warmest thanks to President Wilson for the remarkable promptness with which American aid, in excess of what at one time seemed practicable, has been rendered to the Allies during the past month to meet a great emergency. The crisis, however, still continues. General Foch has presented to us a statement of the utmost gravity, which points out that the numerical superiority of the enemy in France, where 162 Allied divisions now oppose 200 German divisions, is very heavy, and that, as there is no possibility of the British and French increasing the number of their divisions (on the contrary, they are put to extreme straits to keep them up) **there is a great danger of the war being lost** unless the numerical inferiority of the Allies can be remedied as rapidly as possible by the advent of American troops. He, therefore, urges with the utmost insistence that the maximum possible number of infantry and, machine gunners, in which respect the shortage of men on the side of

*the Allies is most marked, should continue to be shipped from America in the months of June and July to **avert the immediate danger of an Allied defeat** in the present campaign owing to the Allied reserves being exhausted before those of the enemy. In addition to this, and looking to the future, he represents that it is **impossible to foresee ultimate victory in the war** unless America is able to provide such an army as will enable the Allies ultimately to establish numerical superiority. We are convinced that General Foch ... is not overestimating the needs of the case ..."[2]*

Even allowing for the Allied military successes on the Western Front in August 1918 which were maintained in the following month, there was little change in the attitude of alarm with which the Allied statesmen viewed the military situation with which they were confronted. A consensus emerged which maintained that victory over the Central Powers was not likely to occur until 1919:

"In British governmental and military circles, the general opinion up to the last few days in September was that outright victory over the Germans was unlikely before 1919, but that dwindling reserves might make a negotiated peace advisable before the winter. Lloyd George did not conceal from the Chief of the Imperial General Staff on the twenty-sixth that he was seriously worried about the manpower situation. Sir Douglas Haig, the British Commander in Chief on the Western Front, declared on August 11, and repeated on September 28, that he would not have enough troops to take the offensive in 1919, and

that therefore the British aim ought to be to go all out to force the Germans to make peace by Christmas. Marshal Foch was convinced that he could beat the Germans in the field, but he did not expect in August to do so before the following summer." [3]

Yet by the end of September 1918 the military situation looked more promising to Allied eyes. In Salonika on 29th September, Germany's ally, Bulgaria, signed an armistice convention with the Allies and, in so doing, exposed the Central Power's southern flank:

"The effect (of this military success) on the minds of the Allied military leaders was profound. On the day of the Macedonian cease-fire Haig told Sir Henry Wilson that he thought the Germans would now ask for peace. A few days later Foch expressed for the first time a lively hope that Germany might crack before the winter." [4]

But the statesmen of Britain, France and Italy were still confronted with one great imponderable, namely, the military capacity of their German opponents. In fact, the military situation confronting the Germans was of such titanic proportions that the Supreme Command, upon receiving news of the collapse of the Macedonian Front, immediately advised its government of the necessity of asking for peace:[5]

"The Supreme Command insists on its demand of Sunday, 29th September, that a peace offer to our enemies be issued at once.

As a result of the collapse of the Macedonian front and the weakening of the Western reserves which

*this has brought about, and now that it is impossible
to make good the very considerable losses which have
been incurred in the battles of the last few days, there
is, so far as can be foreseen, no longer a prospect of
forcing peace on the enemy.*

*The enemy, on the other hand, is continually
bringing new and fresh reserves into the battle.*

*The German army still stands firm and successfully
wards of attacks. But the situation becomes daily
more critical and may force the Supreme Command
to take momentous decisions.*

*It is desirable in the circumstances to break off the
battle in order to spare the Germany people and its
allies useless sacrifices. Every day wasted costs
thousands of brave soldiers their lives."[6]*

Confronted by growing unrest at home and this
evidence of despair of the military situation by the
Supreme Command, Prince Max van Baden had little
option but to seek an ending of hostilities which he did
in a letter to President Wilson on 3rd October 1918:

*"The German Government requests the President of
the United States of America to take in hand the
restoration of peace, to bring this request to the
notice of all belligerent states and to invite them to
send plenipotentiaries for the initiation of
negotiations. They accept as a basis for the peace
negotiations the programme laid down by the
President of the United States of America, in his
message to Congress of 8th January, 1918...*

To avoid further bloodshed, the German Government requests the President to arrange the immediate conclusion of an armistice on land, by sea and in the air."[7]

Although the German note explicitly made reference to peace negotiations taking place on the basis of the Fourteen Points, this should not be taken as unqualified agreement with those points, but is perhaps better interpreted as being the best basis which the Germans could find for negotiation given their parlous military situation and their fear of Bolshevism at home:

"Genuinely eager for an armistice which would give a respite to their army, (the Germans) were nothing like as wholehearted in their desire to make peace on terms dictated by the President. As their situation grew worse, however, a program which seemed to rule out punitive damages and economic sanctions began to look to most of them, though not to all, less unattractive than a further series of battles which were almost certain to turn out badly. Had they been confident that the battles would turn out well, their attitude would have been very different. The Fourteen Points might save them from the worst consequences of unconditional surrender, but they would not particularly favour German interests if they meant that Alsace and Lorraine were to go to France and that Germany was to make sacrifices for the benefit of Poland."[8]

In reality, however, choice was not an option open to the Germans in October 1918:

"... for they were soon in no position to let slip any chance of avoiding defeat in the field and revolution at home. "[9]

Although in a far better position than their German opponents with regard to a choice of the basis upon which an armistice could be negotiated, America's allies were not actors freed of all constraints, neither did they give unreserved acceptance to the Fourteen Points, nor did their acceptance of them come readily. With the arrival in Paris, on 26th October 1918 of Colonel Edward House, President Wilson's confidential adviser, America's allies gradually moved toward acceptance of a peace based on the Fourteen Points. The major difficulty was not the armistice provisions but the final peace settlement and the way in which it could be brought into being:

"Should the Germans be told that they could have peace on the basis of the President's speeches, in accordance with the tentative bargain which they had struck with the United States government, but which did not yet bind anyone since the Allies had not formally assented to it? Or should the Allies openly declare, at the risk of seeing the United States make a separate peace with their enemies, that they would rather enter the peace conference with their hands free? Should they 'hint, ... that a settlement negotiated by the European belligerents without prior commitments to anyone might suit Europe better in the long run than one dictated by the United States ...?"[10]

In his discussion with the statesmen of America's allies, Colonel House was successful in gaining support for the American programme of a peace based on the Fourteen Points for the simple reason that, vis a vis her Allies, the United States was in a strong position and he was not reticent about the implications that their rejection of the American programme would entail:

> *"If they turned down the Fourteen Points, he told the Allied statesmen, then the United States might have to make a separate peace with the Central Powers. Should that happen, the Allies would be left to fight alone if they went on fighting, perhaps deprived of American credit and war materials if they stopped fighting. To reinforce the warning, the President armed his envoy with a specially cabled message threatening to make his disagreement with the Allies public.* "[11]

Such reasoning as this, supported by the threat to invoke sanctions for non-compliance, could hardly have been reassuring to statesmen who gloomily contemplated another year of war in Europe and whose hope of a military victory had been revealed, by their own admission, to be dependent upon the food, war-materials, and troops which were reaching them from across the Atlantic. Faced with such choice as Colonel House's arguments left open to them, America's allies chose acceptance of President Wilson's programme on 5th November 1918, but even then they did so with reservations:

> *"The Allied Governments have given careful consideration to the correspondence which has passed between the President of the United States and the German Government. Subject to the qualifications which follow they declare their*

willingness to make peace with the Government of Germany on the terms of peace laid down in the President's address to Congress of January, 1918, and the principles of settlement enunciated in his subsequent addresses. They must point out, however, that clause 2, relating to what is usually described as the freedom of the seas, is open to various interpretations, some of which they could not accept. They must, therefore, reserve to themselves complete freedom on this subject when they enter the peace conference.

Further, in the conditions of peace laid down in his address to Congress of January 8, 1918, the President declared that invaded territories must be restored as well as evacuated and freed, the Allies feel that no doubt ought to be allowed to exist as to what this provision implies. By it they understand that compensation will be made by Germany for all damage done to the civilian population of the Allies and their property by the aggression of Germany by land, by sea and from the air."[12]

Given that both victors and vanquished arrived at a position in which they had but little choice other than to accept the Fourteen Points as the basis for a peace conference the question must be asked as to the extent to which the Fourteen Points were capable of providing a basis for such a conference to reach a settlement acceptable to both sides. Such a question takes on a more profound significance in the light of post-conference developments.

Robert Lansing, Head of the American Commission at the Paris Conference, left little doubt that in his view the Fourteen Points did not provide a firm foundation upon which a meaningful and lasting peace settlement could be negotiated:

> *"It is hardly worth while to say that the Fourteen Points and the four principles declared in the address of February 11, 1918, do not constitute a sufficient programme for negotiators. Manifestly they are too indefinite in specific application. They were never intended for that purpose when they were proclaimed. They might have formed a general basis for the preparation of instructions for peace commissioners, but they omitted too many of the essentials to be considered actual instructions, while the lack of definitive terms to be included in a treaty further deprived them of that character. Such important and practical subjects as reparations, financial arrangements, the use and control of waterways, and other questions of a like nature, are not even mentioned. As a general statement of the bases of peace the Fourteen Points and subsequent declarations probably served a useful purpose, though some critics would deny this, but as a working programme for the negotiation of a treaty they were inadequate, if not wholly useless."*[13]

Yet even if the Fourteen Points did not provide an adequate basis upon which peace could be negotiated they had themselves to some extent been overtaken by events in Europe in the interim which elapsed between their proclamation and the opening of the Peace Conference in Paris. Perhaps the most important of these events being Allied intervention in Soviet Russia and the increasing political instability which Germany exhibited in the months following the Armistice.

When the Peace Conference opened in Paris the Germans were excluded. They played no part in the deliberations and discussions which took place on the question of the terms of the peace settlement. These were matters which were decided exclusively by the victorious Entente:

> *"The Treaty of Versailles did not assume the form of a pact freely negotiated between the belligerents; it was an instrument imposed by the conquerors upon a crushed and humiliated foe."*[14]

One right was, however, reserved for the defeated Germans, namely, the right to make observations on the draft treaty submitted to them. In making its observations the German delegation took the opportunity to elucidate its anguish at both the general and specific aspects of the draft treaty and to present its own counter-proposals.[15] In its observations the German delegation was unequivocal about the effect which it saw the draft treaty having upon Germany if it were to be implemented:

> *"... the peace document shows that Germany's position as a world power is to be utterly destroyed."*[16]

and

> *"... the draft demands the annexation of purely German territory and the suppression of the German nationality. It involves the utter destruction of German economic life. It leads the German people*

into a financial thraldom unknown in history up to the present day. "[17]

Yet significantly, not only did the German delegation question specific aspects of the draft treaty and offer its own counter-proposals on those, it also questioned the entire legal status of the draft treaty itself. The dubious legality of the draft document was seen by the German delegation as arising from the armistice negotiations initiated by Prince von Baden on 5th October 1918 and which had eventually led to the Armistice of 11th November. The German delegation maintained that there was indisputable evidence that the Armistice negotiations had been based upon an acceptance by both the Entente Powers and its government of President Wilson's Fourteen Points and that those points still constituted the basis of a lasting peace in German eyes:

> *"As a basis of peace, Germany has expressly accepted nothing but President Wilson's fourteen points and his subsequent proclamations. No other bases have been demanded either by President Wilson, or after him, by any of the Allied Governments.*
>
> *The acceptance of the terms of the armistice was, according to President Wilson's own assurance, to be the best evidence of the unequivocal acceptance of the above mentioned fundamental terms and principles of peace on the part of Germany. Germany has accepted the terms of armistice and thereby furnished the proof demanded by President Wilson. Beyond that she has with all her might endeavoured to fulfil those terms in spite of their great severity.*

The Allies have accepted Wilson's fourteen points and his subsequent proclamations as a basis of peace."

A solemn agreement as to the basis of peace therefore exists between the two Contracting Parties. Germany has a right to this basis of peace. By abandoning it the Allies would break an international legal agreement.

"The historical facts stated show that between the German Government on the one hand and the Governments of the Allied and Associated Powers on the other a pactum de contrahendo has been concluded which is, without a doubt, legally binding and whereby the basis for the peace is for both parties unalterably fixed.

The practical application of the principles agreed upon must, according to President Wilson's own words, be the subject of negotiation. Germany has a right to a discussion of the terms of peace. This discussion can only extend to the application of the fourteen points and of the subsequent proclamations of Mr Wilson. If a peace of a different character were to be forced upon Germany, that would be a breach of a solemn pledge.

...the draft of a peace treaty as submitted to the German Government stands in full and irreconcilable conflict with the basis agreed upon for a just and durable peace. Scarcely a single stipulation of the draft corresponds with the conditions agreed upon..." [18]

The Allied reply to the observations of the German delegation on the conditions of peace was, not surprisingly, in sharp contrast to the latter's claim that the Fourteen Points had been omitted from the draft treaty:

> *"The Allied and Associated Powers are in complete accord with the German Delegation in their insistence that the basis for the negotiation of a treaty of peace is to be found in the correspondence which immediately preceded the signing of the armistice of November 11, 1918. It was there agreed that the treaty of peace should be based upon the fourteen points of President Wilson's address of January 8, 1918, as they were modified by the Allies' memorandum included in the President's note of November 5, 1918, and upon the principles of settlement enunciated by President Wilson in his later addresses ... These are the principles upon which hostilities were abandoned in November 1918, these are the principles upon which the Allied and Associated Powers agreed that peace might be based, these are the principles which have guided them in the deliberations which have led to the formulation of the conditions of peace."[19]*

To the German claim that,

> *"The peace to be concluded with Germany was to be a peace of right, not a peace of might."[20]*

The Allies replied that,

> *"The Allied and Associated Powers believe that they will be false to those who have given their all to save the freedom of the world if they consent to treat this*

war on any other basis than as a crime against humanity and right ...Justice, therefore, is the only possible basis for the settlement of the accounts of this terrible war. Justice is what the German Delegation ask for and say that Germany has been promised. Justice is what Germany shall have. But it must be justice for all. There must be justice for the dead and wounded and for those who have been orphaned and bereaved that Europe might be freed from Prussian despotism. There must be justice for the peoples who now stagger under war debts which exceed £30,000,000,000 that liberty might be saved. There must be justice for those millions whose homes and land, ships and property German savagery has spoliated and destroyed.

That is why the Allied and Associated Powers have insisted as a cardinal feature of the treaty that Germany must undertake to make reparations to the very uttermost of her power; for reparations for wrongs inflicted is of the essence of. justice... That, too, is why Germany must submit for a few years to certain special disabilities and arrangements ... If these things are hardships for Germany, they are hardships which Germany has brought upon herself. Somebody must suffer for the consequences of the war. Is it to be Germany, or only the peoples she has wronged?"

Not to do justice to all concerned would only leave the world open to fresh calamities...

"The Allied and Associated Powers therefore believe that the peace they have proposed is fundamentally a

peace of justice. They are no less certain that it is a
peace of right fulfilling the terms agreed upon at the
time of the armistice." [21]

Although the Alied reply seemed harsh and unsympathetic in the tenor it struck in response to the German delegation's observations certain concessions were made, notably in the re-adjustment of the eastern borders of Germany and the holding of a plebiscite to determine the future possession of Upper Silesia. With these amendments included, the Treaty of Versailles was signed on 28th June 1919.

In virtually every way the post-Versailles Germany was but a poor relation of the pre-war Germany with territorial changes arising at virtually all points of her previous boundaries. In the south the territorial changes were minimal with small areas of land being ceded to Belgium, whilst in the north changes of a slightly greater magnitude took place with northern Schleswig being incorporated into Denmark as a result of a plebiscite.[22] The territorial changes were, however, more dramatic in the west and in the east. In the west the provinces of Alsace and Lorraine which had come into German possession in 1871 were returned to France whilst the Saar Basin was separated from Germany and placed under a League of Nations commission pending a plebiscite in fifteen years time.[23] Of greater import were the territorial changes in the east where West Prussia was incorporated into the new Polish state, Upper Silesia was divided between Germany and Poland as a result of a plebiscite and the former German City of Danzig was established as a Free City and placed under the protection of the League of Nations whilst also serving as a port for Poland, access to which was secured by means of a "Polish Corridor" which effectively severed East Prussia from the rest of Germany. For similar reasons, the city of Memel was granted to the newly created state of Lithuania.[24] Nor was Germany's colonial empire spared from change. Germany's African colonies were shared between Britain, France, Belgium and South Africa whilst those in the Pacific were divided between Japan, Australia, Britain and New Zealand.[25]

In addition to territorial questions the Treaty of Versailles was also concerned with the issues of reparations, the demilitarisation of the Rhineland, disarmament, and the provision of guarantees for Germany's compliance with the obligations placed upon her. The question of reparations was one of the most contentious issues of the Paris Conference as too large a sum could have resulted in Germany refusing to sign the treaty, whilst a sum likely to be within Germany's capacity to pay might have proved unacceptable to public opinion in both France and Britain.[26] In the event, no total sum was set in the treaty for reparations nor was there any limitation placed upon the number of years during which Germany was to make payment.[27] Part VIII of the Treaty of Versailles which dealt with the question of reparations also contained Article 231 which entailed an admission of Germany's guilt for the war:

"The Allied and Associated Governments affirm and Germany accepts the responsibility of Germany and her allies for causing all of the loss and damage to which the Allied and Associated Governments and their nationals have been subjected as a consequence

of the war imposed upon them by the aggression of Germany and her allies."

Further, under Part V of the treaty, Germany was forbidden to maintain any fortifications or armed forces on either side of the banks of the Rhine for a distance of 50 kilometres, and was obliged to limit her army to one hundred thousand men, to abolish compulsory military service, to restrict her naval forces and to have no air force or submarines. Finally, as a guarantee for compliance with the treaty, the German territory west of the Rhine, together with the bridgeheads was to be occupied by Allied and Associated troops for a period of fifteen years. In effect the military provisions rendered Germany virtually defenceless from outside aggression and capable only of the maintenance of law and order within her boundaries.[28]

Germany emerged from the Paris Conference a greatly weakened and deeply embittered nation.

Although Germany presented problems to the peacemakers at Paris and allowing for the fact that their subsequent decisions gave rise to a deep seated sense of grievance among the German politicians and people at the treatment they had received, Russia presented a problem of at least comparable, if not greater, magnitude and complexity:

"The effect of the Russian problem on the Paris Conference ... was profound. Paris cannot be understood without Moscow. Without ever being represented at Paris at all, the Bolsheviki and Bolshevism were powerful elements at every turn. Russia played a more vital part at Paris than Prussia! For the Prussian idea had been utterly

defeated, while the Russian idea was still rising in power."[29]

"The peacemakers themselves attached considerable importance to the Russian operation. In preparing for the conference they placed Russian affairs high on its agenda. The Russian problem cropped up repeatedly during the consultations among the Western Statesmen before the opening of the conference. In the first two weeks of the conference the Allied rulers spent more time discussing Russia than any other subject, and they returned to it frequently during the remainder of the conference."[30]

Russia had become a problem, both militarily and politically, to the Entente in November 1917 when the Bolsheviks seized power in the October Revolution:

"Here was a military problem on such a scale that it dwarfed all the other setbacks of the year, and it goes far to explain the Allied desperation and sense of outrage. At the same time they were faced with a political problem as complex as it was urgent. Russia was out of the war but not out of existence. Could any thing be salvaged from the wreckage? This raised the question of whether or not to recognise the new regime."[31]

With the coming into effect of the Armistice on 11th November 1918 the argument for Allied troops to be employed in Russia as a means of maintaining an eastern front was rendered fallacious.[32] It is possible to question whether or not the Allies were ever in a position to maintain an eastern front in being at any time prior to the Armistice and, in consequence, other motives have been attributed to their decision to send troops to Russia.[33] Yet, as Thompson notes, prior to the Armistice:

> "Allied intervention seems clearly to have been chiefly motivated by strategic considerations of the all-out struggle with Germany, no matter how chimerical and vain such calculations appear in retrospect."[34]

Even so, in January 1919, two months after the Armistice came into effect, Russia was engaged on virtually all of her frontiers with opponents largely supported by her former allies:

> "At Omsk, in Siberia, the anti-Soviet Admiral Kolchak was established, endeavouring, with American and Japanese assistance, to push westwards across the Uralsto join hands with an anti-Soviet Archangel Government resting on British, American and Italian bayonets. At Murmansk, another Allied expedition was based on Northern Russia's only warm-water port. General Yudenitch did not begin his march on Petrograd till later in the year; but in the Baltic region Germans were supporting the local troops, Estonians and Letts, against the Bolsheviks. Poland was doing her best to drive her eastern frontier deeper into Russia. In the Ukraine Petliura, who had lately obtained chief power, was threatening Russia's western government. And in the Crimea, General Denikin, with Allied fleets to supply him and guard his rear, was driving toward the basin of the Don."[35]

In the light of this military adventure it is worthwhile considering the attitudes of the victorious major western powers toward Russia at the opening of the Paris Peace Conference. The attitude of the United States government contained three elements, namely, non-recognition of the Soviet government, non-intervention in Russia's internal affairs, and preservation of Russia's territorial integrity:[36]

> "... non recognition of the Soviet government was based on the argument that no government should be recognised unless it represented the will of the people. Non intervention and the commitment to Russia's territorial integrity stemmed from Wilson's conviction that the Russian people should be permitted to settle their own affairs and to determine their own future."[37]

Although non-intervention was a key element in the attitude of the United States government toward Russia, American troops had been dispatched into Siberia and Northern Russia but their presence on Soviet soil was justified by the contention that they were a means of aiding the Russian people in attaining self-government, a justification in accord with the sixth of President Wilson's Fourteen Points.[38] As to the sort of Russia which the Americans thought would eventually emerge there was disagreement. If President Wilson favoured the maintenance of a new Russia with boundaries compatible with those of the Czarist Russia it had replaced, there was also those, such as Robert Lansing and Colonel House, who favoured the break-up of Russia into a number of smaller, autonomous republics.[39]

Likewise, in the British government, there was no clear consensus to emerge over the Russian problem. The pro-interventionists, notably among whom were Lord Curzon, Lord Milner and Winston Churchill, were of the opinion that Bolshevism represented a threat not only to their own country but also to the countries of Central Europe and that, in consequence, it should be suppressed by military means whilst at the same time contending that Britain owed a debt to those in Russia who, unlike the Bolsheviks, had opposed the Germans and were now engaged in opposing the latter.[40] In contrast to the pro-interventionists were those who like Lloyd George, on occasions, and Arthur Balfour, more consistently, were doubtful of the returns which would accrue from direct intervention or from support for the various anti-Bolshevik forces and factions. Balfour, in particular,

> "... felt that food relief and the settlement of political and territorial questions which were exciting popular passions would suffice to eliminate the danger of Bolshevism by building up a cordon of new states in Central and Eastern Europe."[41]

The attitude of Lloyd George did little to assist the formulation of a comprehensive and consistent British policy toward Russia:

> "As a liberal, he believed that the aspirations of the Bolsheviks were not entirely unworthy, whatever their policies...(he) was convinced ... that the Russian people should be allowed to settle their own affairs ....
> As a humanitarian, the British leader was genuinely anxious to bring peace to Russia ... as a politician (he) was quick to adapt his Russian policy to the

prevailing political winds ... In sum, Lloyd George's Russian policy was capricious and inconsistent, reflecting the conflict between his personal preferences and his political calculations."[42]

If Lloyd George's fear of Bolshevism did not amount to that of some of his colleagues, traditional British interests ensured that a powerful post-war Russia was unacceptable to the British government. Firstly, there was the long standing threat which Russia had been seen to pose to British interests in the Far East, Central Asia and Persia. Secondly, there was the fear that, in the presence of a defeated and weakened Germany, a strong Russia, either alone or in concert with France, could destroy the ability of Britain to play the role of "balancer" with regard to Europe; a role which she had long coveted and seen herself as playing. [43]

If there was little by way of a coherent Russian policy emanating from Washington and London the same could also be said of Paris but to a rather lesser extent. French attitudes toward Russia comprised three elements which were often pursued simultaneously even though, to some extent, those elements could be said to be incompatible:

"The most important French objective in Eastern Europe, the one which was most insistently and unwaveringly striven for and on which French policy ultimately came firmly to rest, was the creation of a string of buffer states in that area - especially Poland, Rumania, and Czechoslovakia - closely allied to France and with sufficient viability and combined strength to replace Russia as a

counterweight to Germany and to serve as a barrier, both against possible German expansion eastward and against any future intrusion of Russian power into Europe. Next among French goals was the restoration of a strong Russia to include most of the former empire but not Bessarabia and the Polish territories. A Russia reconstituted in this way would be intimately linked to France and would again play its former role of balancing Germany in the East. Finally, the French considered off and on during 1918 and early 1919, but rejected by the spring of 1919, the possibility of supplementing their basic cordon of East European allies with a few small,. French-dominated states carved out of Russia, such as the Ukraine and the Crimea. These, it was believed, would not only serve French political interests, but also provide a fertile field for French economic and commercial activity." [44]

Of the three victorious major European powers Italy had least interest in the problem posed by Russia, if for no other reason than any dismemberment of the former Czarist Empire was unlikely to result in her making territorial gains; of greater interest to her was the fate of the former Ottoman Empire. Yet the Italian government, faced with political and economic problems at home, was ostensibly anti-Bolshevik in outlook but,

"At the same time the Italians were half-hearted in their support of intervention, although later, in the spring of 1919, they were willing, almost anxious, to take a hand in events in the Caucasus, apparently seeing an opportunity to intrude Italian influence in that oil-rich area ... but reluctant to commit any

Italian resources to intervention, recognising that such a venture would be expensive, as well as unpopular among their people, and that they could supply no reliable troops."[45]

So, on the eve of the Paris Conference it appeared that the major western powers who were to play the decisive role in the proceedings of the Conference were unable to produce any comprehensive policy toward Soviet Russia. Both individually and collectively their Russian policy was marked by disagreement and dissension, with short term measures outweighing long term considerations. But underlying this apparent incongruity were two shared assumptions:

"... that the wicked Soviet regime could not last, and that Allied power could shape the course of affairs in Russia. Both were, of course, utterly false ..."[46]

When the Paris Peace Conference first opened the German question, although very much a problem to the Allied statesmen in terms of the exact requirements which were to be placed upon Germany, was a less complex problem than that which Russia presented. To begin with, there was the question of Russian representation at the Conference:

"So far as Germany was concerned, the Conference was predicated on the unconditional surrender which had been the goal of all Allied policy in the final months of the war. The German people, it was argued, should not even have a voice in the forming of the peace; they would take what they got. But how about the Russian people? In Russia, hostilities had not ceased. In Russia, on the Bolshevik side, there

was still open hostility, scorn, recalcitrance, with regard to Allied purposes. Despite numerous Allied expressions of friendship for the Russian people, there was no Russian representative to take part in the proceedings of the conference. Germany, then, was absent from the discussion at Paris because the Allies wished her to be absent; Russia was absent because there was a virtual state of war between the Allied governments and the effective power in Russia. "[47]

According to Kennan, Wilson and Lloyd George were in favour of permitting Russian representation at the Conference whilst Clemenceau was outrightly opposed to such a measure,[48] yet Thompson contends that the representation of Russia at the Conference was opposed by all three statesmen, although Wilson and Lloyd George did go so far as to favour the major western powers receiving, in Paris, delegations from all shades of political opinion both within and without Russia.[49] In reality, the true position falls somewhere between the two with Wilson and Lloyd George shifting from Russian representation at the Conference proper to a meeting in Paris with the various Russian factions in the face of opposition to the former idea from Clemenceau.

But the question of Russian representation at Paris was not simply a matter of dispute between the leading western statesmen, it was also a problem in international law:

"Among the questions which puzzled the diplomats, both White Russian and Allied, were the following: Since the Allies had not recognised the Soviet

government or the Treaty of Brest-Litovsk, was not Russia still a cobelligerent in the war? If so, was she not entitled to sit at the peace conference to protect her interests and to claim her rights? On the other hand, the Provisional Government of 1917 no longer existing, what group or individual of the many struggling against the Bolsheviks could represent Russia? In any case, had not Russia as a sovereign entity defaulted her claims growing out of the war and the secret treaties when the Bolsheviks deserted the Allied cause and published those treaties? Moreover, what of the Fourteen Points on which the peace was to be based? They referred to a future Russian government representing the will of the Russian people and seemed to supercede the secret treaties. Finally, had not consideration to be given, under the principle of self-determination, to the desires and interests of the minority peoples of the former Russian empire?"[50]

Although a Russian Political Conference was eventually formed comprising the majority of anti-Bolshevik shades of political opinion and interests, this body was not given official representation at the Conference;[51] the Peace Conference Rules and Regulations presented to the first plenary session on 18th January 1919 stated that,

"The conditions of the representation of Russia shall be fixed by the Conference at the moment when the matters concerning Russia are examined."[52]

But even when "matters concerning Russia" were examined they were examined in the absence of any formal Russian representative, even though Russia was a constantly recurring theme throughout the Conference. In fact, there were five different attempts made during the course of the Conference to resolve the problem which Russia presented. The first of these, given that at no time had it been formally agreed that the Bolsheviks should be invited to Paris either to attend the Conference or for unofficial discussions, was an invitation to all of the warring factions in Russia to send representatives, by 1st February 1919, to a conference on the island of Prinkipo in the Sea of Marmara where they could meet with Allied representatives. Practical and idealistic considerations both necessitated a meeting between the various Russian factions, especially the Bolsheviks, and the statesmen of the Western Powers.[53]

At the idealistic level, the proposal was intended to bring about agreement between the various competing factions in Russia as this was seen as necessary to ensure the well-being of the Russian people in that it would have afforded them the opportunity to produce a government of their own choosing; thus the Prinkipo proposal corresponded to the principle of self-determination contained in the Fourteen Points and received support from the liberal and socialist elements in the Western States.[54] At the practical level the Prinkipo proposal could be seen as enabling the re-integration of Russia into the world political system whilst her absence from the community of states considerably lessened the prospects of a new world order being established along Wilsonian lines and reduced the possibility of a lasting peace.[55] Furthermore,

> "On the practical side, the conclusion of the war
> made it impossible any longer to depict intervention
> as an anti-German measure ... Much of public
> opinion opposed its continuation, and Allied soldiers
> objected to fighting in Russia. At the same time,
> there was a growing conviction among many British
> and American officials, including Lloyd George and
> Wilson, that the existing, half-hearted intervention
> was ineffectual, and served only to arouse Russian
> patriotism against the West and to strengthen the
> hand of the Bolsheviks. Moreover, those observers
> distrusted the politics and principles of the anti-
> Bolshevik leaders and governments and doubted the
> ultimate success of the White Russian cause."[56]

In the event, the Prinkipo proposal came to nothing.
The reasons for this can be attributed to a number of
factors among which must have been the refusal of the
White Russians to attend the proposed meeting because
of their detestation of the Bolsheviks, their fears that the
former Russian Empire would be in some way
dismembered and their rather questionably based belief
that they were capable of inflicting military defeat upon
the Bolshevik forces.[57] In addition, it must not be
overlooked that there was little Allied pressure put on
the White Russians to send representatives to Prinkipo
and that this absence of pressure may be attributed to
the disagreement among the major powers as to the
wisdom of calling for such a meeting to take place at all;
the French were enthusiastic in their encouragement of
the various anti-Bolshevik factions not to accept the
invitation.[58] Furthermore, there was in the Bolshevik
acceptance of the invitation, phraseology offensive to
the extenders of the invitation and which only served to

undermine their faith in the possibility of the proposed meeting being productive.[59] Also, there was the fact that the Bolshevik acceptance failed to mention the call for a truce which was the basic provision underlying the invitation.[60] Finally, and in some ways perhaps of greatest importance, was the fact that the differences between the White Russians and the Bolsheviks were non-negotiable; a factor which appeared to have escaped the notice of the majority of the statesmen of the Western Powers.[61]

With the demise of the Prinkipo proposal, a second course of action to resolve the Russian problem was considered at Paris. This was,

> "... a brief and valiant personal effort by Mr Winston Churchill to bring things to a head and to compel the Bolsheviki either to cease hostilities at once or to suffer a greatly increased Allied military effort against them."[62]

Political difficulties at home had necessitated Lloyd George's departure from Paris and with the departure of President Wilson to the United States, for a period of several weeks, imminent, it would seem that the British Cabinet reached the decision to send Churchill to Paris.[63] Certainly other considerations occasioned that decision such as the failure of the Prinkipo proposal and opposition in the Cabinet to Lloyd George's doubts about the efficacy of Allied intervention in Russia. The fact that it was Churchill who went to Paris would seem to imply that those members of the British government favouring a military solution to the Russian problem had, at least temporarily, gained the ascendancy. How it was decided that it should be Churchill who went to the

Conference remains unclear, especially given that Churchill and Lloyd George were advocating incompatible solutions to the problem which Russia posed:

> "... *the most formidable and irrepressible protagonist of an anti-Bolshevik war was Mr Winston Churchill.*"[64]

whilst,

> "*(Lloyd George) was definitely opposed to military intervention in any shape.*"[65]

Lloyd George was later to be damning in his criticism of this attempt by Churchill to swing the Paris Conference on to the path of large scale military intervention by the Allies in Russia:

> "*Mr Churchill very adroitly seized the opportunity ... to go over to Paris and urge **his plans** with regard to Russia upon the consideration of the French, the American and the British delegations.* "[66]

The major thrust of Churchill's argument in favour of an all-out Allied military enterprise in Russia was that this course of action was necessary to eradicate the ambiguity which had resulted from the failure of the Prinkipo proposal.[67] Churchill,

> "*pointed particularly to the deterioration of the military situation of the anti-Bolshevik forces in Russia and to the weakened morale of the Allied units there ... (and) the debt of loyalty the Allies owed to the anti-Bolshevik forces with whom they were associated.*"[68]

In his response to this line of argument Wilson made mention of the fact that the Allied troops seemed to be doing little good in Russia, that they were unsure as to their purpose in being there, that the groups they were supporting gave no sign of political promise, and that since the Allied forces would have to leave Russia someday it might as well be sooner as later.[69] As an alternative scheme Wilson,

> "hinted at the desirability of getting in touch with the Soviet leaders through informal representatives."[70]

Yet Churchill was not without support in his advocacy of a military solution to the problem of Russia via increased Allied intervention:

> "There can be no doubt that the French military authorities, with the full propagandist support of the press of the Right in France, were anxious to organise active military intervention in Russia."[71]

and during Lloyd George's absence, a scheme was put forward by Marshall Foch to the Council of Four which proposed,

> " ...a vast attack on Soviet Russia by Finns, Estonians, Letts, Lithuanians, Poles, Czechs, Russians - in fact, all the peoples that lie along the borders of Russia - all under Allied direction."[72]

Despite further efforts by Churchill to gain acceptance for a military crusade against Bolshevism after Wilson's return to the United States, intensified intervention was effectively discounted by the Conference.[73]

A considerable difficulty which was implicit in any attempt to resolve the Russian problem was the absence of reliable information about the existing situation in Russia and the views of the Soviet leadership:

> "We did not know the facts about Russia. Differing reports were received from our representatives in Russia, and often reports from the same representative varied from day to day. It was clear that, unless we knew the facts, we should not be in a position to form a correct judgment."[74]

The problem of a lack of reliable and consistent information, coupled with Wilson's suggestion that the views of the Soviet leadership be sought through the medium of informal representatives, may be seen as the catalyst which produced the third approach to the Russian problem which the statesmen at Paris undertook, namely,

> "...an attempt by the American and British governments to sound out the Soviet leaders by sending a secret diplomatic agent, Mr William C Bullitt, to Moscow to talk to them."[75]

Such a course of action was completely compatible with the ill-fated Prinkipo proposal which had preceded it in that Prinkipo owed much to the desire of Wilson and Lloyd George to hear all sides of Russian political opinion both within and without Russia, but especially the views of the Bolsheviks. Given this, and the French opposition to Prinkipo and their championing of the anti-Bolshevik cause, it cannot be surprising that the Americans did not inform their French counterparts of Bullitt's mission.[76] Although the Bullitt mission had originally been conceived as an investigative one, its purpose was broadened, largely at the instigation of Colonel House, to include the conduct of negotiations with the Soviet government.[77] Whichever view is taken of the mission's brief, Bullitt himself was in no doubt as to its purpose,

> "...I was instructed to go in and bring back as quickly as possible a definitive statement of exactly the terms the Soviet Government was ready to accept. The idea in the minds of the British and American delegations were that if the Allies made another proposal it should be a proposal which we would know in advance would be accepted, so that there would be no chance of another Prinkipo proposal miscarrying."[78]

That Bullitt was given a negotiating role would appear to be irrefutable as he was provided with a series of points which could be included in any settlement with the Soviet government. From Colonel House, four points emerged, a cease-fire, an amnesty for pro-Allied Russians, restoration of trade, and an equitable distribution of relief supplies.[79] From Philip Kerr, Lloyd George's Private Secretary, an additional eight points originated, namely,

> "...de facto governments to remain in control of the territories they occupied, regulation of railways and ports in accord with international agreements, right of free entry and full security for Allied subjects in Soviet Russia, amnesty for all political prisoners on both sides, separate consideration of the debt question following the establishment of peace, and the withdrawal of Allied troops after the

demobilisation of Russian armies to a line to be defined."[80]

The domestic and external situations with which the Soviet leadership were confronted would appear to have held out some hope for the success of the Bullitt mission:

"(The) situation had improved only slightly, if at all, since Lenin's decision in the fall of 1918 to attempt to secure peace with the Allies at almost any cost and since the conciliatory reply of the Soviet government to the Prinkipo invitation a month earlier, when substantial concessions were offered the Western governments. Soviet Russia still faced a ring of external enemies. The Red Army had achieved some successes in the Ukraine and was advancing in the Baltic area; on the other hand, Denikin had improved his position in south Russia. The economic crisis was, if anything, worse, the supply of food and fuel to Moscow itself being reduced to a trickle conditions of economic stagnation and virtual starvation ... prevailed."[81]

After a series of meetings with, in particular, Lenin, Chicherin and Litvinov, Bullitt had, by 12th March 1919 secured a set of proposals agreed by the Bolshevik Central Committee:

"The proposals were in the form of an offer to be made by the Allies. The Soviet government agreed to accept this offer provided it was made not later than April 10th. The major provisions of the offer followed rather closely the outline terms given Bullitt by Kerr. The Allies were to propose a two week armistice on all fronts ... A peace conference would then be convened in a neutral country .."[82]

Despite the promise which it seemed to entail, the Bullitt mission came to nothing. A number of reasons may be advanced for the failure of the statesmen at Paris to develop the openings which Bullitt's talks with the Soviet Leadership had created. Firstly, there was the attitude of Wilson and Lloyd George:

"The explanation of Wilson's failure to support Bullitt's recommendations would seem ... to lie in his attitude toward the Russian question at the time. The bits of evidence available indicate that insofar as Wilson had a policy on Russia at that moment, it was to do nothing"[83]

and:

"it seems clear that Wilson showed no enthusiasm for the Soviet proposals ..."[84]

whilst Lloyd George found it,

"...politically awkward for him to espouse a moderate course toward Russia in the face of violently anti-Bolshevik British opinion..."[85]

The failure of the Bullitt mission can also be attributed to the fact that,

"...the Western leaders, and especially Wilson, were too preoccupied to give Bullitt's proposals the careful consideration they deserved (and that) they, and especially Lloyd George, were so influenced by conservative opinion in the press and among the public that they were prevented from taking a bold *step, which, though undoubtedly unpopular in some circles, would probably have been in the best interests of the West."[86]*

Other reasons have, however, also to be taken into account. There was, for instance, the political composition of the small party which accompanied Bullitt to Moscow, which was lacking in anyone in whom the anti-Bolshevik groups in the west could place their faith and whose judgment they could trust:

"Although the composition of the mission undoubtedly helped ensure Bullitt a sympathetic reception from the Soviet leaders, it had just the reverse effect on many individuals at the peace conference and on conservative legislative and press circles in England and America."[87]

In addition, the secretive manner in which the Bullitt mission was formulated and its unofficial status cast a shadow over the possibility of its findings and proposals being given credibility:

"Overall, it seems clear that in Paris Colonel House of the American delegation and Kerr and Sir Maurice Hankey of the British delegation knew what terms Bullitt was planning to propose to the Soviet leaders. President Wilson certainly did not, in fact, he was probably even unaware, until after his return to Paris from Washington, that House had empowered Bullitt to negotiate, as well as to investigate."[88]

and

"Very few of the British government knew of the mission .... The Foreign Office itself did not, and, in fact, it did not learn the details of the affair until four months later ...Nor was the British War Office notified of Bullitt's trip when he departed ... news of the departure was kept from the press."[89]

Finally, two further factors have to be considered which rendered the Bullitt mission fruitless, namely, the fact that a new initiative on Russia was being actively considered during Bullitt's absence in Moscow which entailed the provision of food relief to Russia from the West. Secondly, and perhaps in some ways the most important of all the reasons which could be thought of for the failure of the Bullitt mission, namely, the fact that Bullitt, by returning to Paris from Moscow with so rigid a set of proposals,

"...left to the Allied governments no latitude of negotiation. By taking cognisance of the document, they would obviously place themselves in a position where they could only take it or leave it. Any alteration in its text at the Allied end would have given the Soviet government formal grounds for refusing to accept it."[90]

By the time of Bullitt's return to Paris, active consideration was being given to a food relief programme for Russia which, it was anticipated, would have as its outcome the end of the civil war in Russia on terms favourable to Allied interests:[91]

"Whether this would involve the fall of the Soviet regime was ... not clear in the minds of most people who entertained the idea; but it was assumed that at

least the Russian Communists could be confronted with the choice between moderating their behaviour and their principles of conduct, or accepting the onus of denying the proffered food to a Russian population, large parts of which were already starving."[92]

One of the prime movers of this initiative was Herbert Hoover, whose experience in running such a programme was extensive, having himself been Director of the Commission for Relief in Belgium [93] and at the time of the Paris Conference he was Food Administrator for all Allied relief enterprises. Food relief as a means of resolving the Russian problem, although standing in marked contrast to military intervention in Russia, had certain advantages:

"Since the money and food would be donated by Americans, the action could always be portrayed to people at home as an altruistic and benevolent one, and made to contrast favourably with that evil and awful thing called 'power politics' of which the European countries were presumed to be chronically guilty. No use of force was involved. No troops had to be kept on foreign soil as sanctions of this diplomacy. One was relieved of the sordid ordeal of political negotiations and compromise. One simply defined ones conditions and left it to the other fellow to take it. If he accepted, all right; if he declined, so much the worse for him."[94]

Additionally, it could be argued that relief avoided the question or not to give official recognition to the Bolsheviks and, if as Hoover had proposed, the relief agency was headed by a member of a neutral state, it would avoid any direct dealings between the Western Powers and the Bolsheviks,

> *"In a sense the relief programme . . . represented a compromise between a policy of further intervention and the idea of reaching an accommodation with the Bolsheviks."*[95]

The idea of a food relief programme was not suggested for the first time at the Peace Conference, and its likelihood of success was increased by reports of starvation which were emanating from Russia.[96] In the event, Fridtjof Nansen accepted the leadership of the proposed relief agency for Russia[97] and by the 17th April 1919 had secured the permission of the Council of Four for a message to be sent to the Bolsheviks. As with other proposals at the Conference designed to resolve the Russian problem there was an absence of any deep seated consensus about the efficacy of the relief programme among the Western Powers; the French, in particular, expressed grave doubt about its desirability.[98]

The conditions governing the relief offer were hardly likely to have been well received in Moscow stipulating, as they did, a cessation of hostilities in Russia, that the distribution and transportation of the relief supplies within Russia were to be under the supervision of the proposed Relief Commission, and that subject to this supervision the distribution of food at the local level was to be solely under the control of the Russian people themselves. In addition, no mention was made of the withdrawal of Allied forces from Russia.[99] As Kennan notes,

"The provision for supervision of all Russian transportation by the Relief Commission meant simply taking one great and vital branch of economic and military administration out of the hands of the Russian government entirely. This the Soviet government could never have accepted without a disastrous collapse of its prestige. But beyond this, how could the people of any Russian locality act as a collective entity in such matters, even assuming that experience and tradition had fitted them to do so, unless they were in some way organised and represented for this purpose? This meant elections - elections of public bodies with real power. But the Russia of the spring 1919 was, God knows, in no condition to conduct elections of any kind. It was ravaged by hunger and cold and confusion and a civil war which had now advanced to the utmost degree of bitterness and commitment on both sides. Who was to organise such elections? Who was to stand guard over their impartiality? Who was to see and count the ballots? Where was the Russian whose detachment towards the civil war was so great and so generally recognised that others would consent to place their lives and that of their families in his power by handing him a secret ballot? The very suggestion of local community action of this sort reflected a terrifying naivete as to what the Russia of that hour was really like. [100]

Likewise, Thompson observes that,

"The spectacle of the Allied heads of government solemnly endorsing a plan which, besides its humanitarian aspects, provided for considerable

interference in Russia's economic and political life,
and then being unable or unwilling even to transmit
the message to the Bolsheviks reflected the illusory
nature of the whole affair and boded ill for its
success."[101]

Not surprisingly, the Bolsheviks found that the conditions imposed upon the offer of food relief made their acceptance of that offer an impossibility. Chicherin replied direct to Nansen denouncing the Allied note and contending that the provision of a cease-fire was simply a trick to prevent a Bolshevik victory in the civil war which would ensue if no further increase in Allied military intervention took place.[102] To this extent Chicherin conceived the Allied proposal to be a political and not a humanitarian act. In short, the Allied conditions were unacceptable to the Bolsheviks, although the latter were prepared to meet with Nansen on neutral territory to discuss the implementation of relief work in Russia, and they were also prepared to meet directly with the Allied Powers to discuss the cessation of hostilities in Russia and the possibility of arranging a settlement to end both the civil war and Allied intervention.[103]

Chicherin's reply to Nansen excited little interest at the Paris Conference largely because of reports from Russia that the military situation in the civil war there had dramatically altered.[104] Admiral Kolchak's anti-Bolshevik forces had, during March and April 1919, produced a string of military successes which implied that the Bolsheviks were approaching defeat and that Kolchak would soon be in control of most of Russia:[105]

When news of Kolchak's successes reached Paris, the Big Four were only too glad to drop the whole question of food relief and to pin their hopes for a solution of the Russian question on the triumph of the anti-Bolshevik forces and the elimination of the Soviet regime.

After a brief, hesitant impulse toward an approach to the Russian problem through the relief, the pendulum of conference policy was (by March 1919) once again to the anti-Bolshevik side, where it was to remain for many months."[106]

Until the Autumn of 1919 the Allies placed force foremost among the measures likely to resolve the Russian problem and encouraged by the reports reaching Paris of Admiral Kolchak's successes against the Bolsheviks he became the centre of their hopes. Proposed support for Kolchak had, however, been voiced earlier than May 1919. British and French officials had, as early as December 1918, advocated such a course of action and British enthusiasm had led them in March 1919 to renew their suggestion that this be done.[107] In addition, having ruled out direct Allied military intervention and having met with scant encouragement over the Prinkipo proposal and the food relief programme from the Bolsheviks, the statesmen at Paris had become convinced that there was little prospect of resolving the Russian problem by dealing directly with the Bolsheviks.[108] After some hesitation it was agreed by the Council of Four plus Japan that support for Kolchak offered the most feasible course of action and by 26th May 1919 these five powers resolved to support Kolchak subject to his compliance with a number of conditions which they saw fit to place upon him and the government which he had established at Omsk [109] The conditions were,

> ...*that immediately upon reaching Moscow (Kolchak and his associates) would either organise the 'free, secret, and democratic' election of a constituent assembly or summon the Assembly of 1917 as a stopgap; that until then they would allow free elections 'for all local and legally constituted assemblies such as municipalities and Zemstvos'; that they would 'not revive the special privileges of any class or order' nor restore the 'former land system'; that they would support civil and religious liberty, and would not 'reintroduce the regime which the revolution had destroyed'; and that they would recognise the independence of Finland and Poland; that Russia's relations with the border territories would be settled 'in consultation and cooperation' with the League; that Russia's international debts would be honoured; and they 'would undertake to form a single government and army command' as soon as possible."*[110]

Agreement to these conditions having been received from Kolchak, he was assured by the Big Five [111] of aid in his struggle against the Bolsheviks.[112] Yet Allied support for Kolchak fell short of de facto recognition of his government as the government of all Russia. [113]

Although support for Kolchak produced a greater degree of unanimity among the statesmen at Paris than did any of their other initiatives in response to the problem which Russia presented, it was doomed to failure at the very moment at which it was being decided, for during June 1919 Kolchak's forces had been held by the Bolsheviks and were never able to recapture their forwardmomentum and by the autumn of 1919 they had collapsed.[114]

Whilst it is relatively easy to highlight the reasons behind the failure of each of the specific policies which the Western statesmen arrived at during the Peace Conference it is, perhaps, a little too simplistic to suggest that they failed completely in their opposition to Bolshevism:

> *"These efforts were partially successful: although the Soviet regime in Russia was not destroyed, it was temporarily checked from extending its control over the nonRussian areas on the Western borders of the former Tsarist Empire."[115]*

Also, it must be questioned whether the statesmen at Paris could realistically have been expected to do much more than they did bearing in mind the constraints under which they had to operate:

> *"It is hardly surprising that the statesmen in Paris, hampered by insufficient authority, power, and popular support and frequently confronted with conflicting interests among the Allied powers and between the White Russians and the non-Russian border peoples, were unable to develop a clearer and more consistent policy toward Russia than the vague anti-Bolshevism the conference espoused or to coordinate effectively Western policy and the varied aspects of the anti-Bolshevik movement. Whether a better organised and more concerted effort might have toppled the Soviet regime is problematical.*

In any case, the result was a statement between the West and Soviet Russia. With the collapse of the forces of Kolchak, Denikin and Yudenich in the late fall of 1919, it was clear that indirect intervention in Russia ... had failed. The Soviet government was isolated but undefeated. The border peoples seemed on the verge of securing a precarious independence.... Bolshevism had survived, and the Allied leaders now had to decide how the West could live with it."[116]

In the closing weeks of the Paris Conference, the Allied statesmen made the adjustment to an acceptance of a Bolshevik Russia in the most ambivalent of ways:

"On the one hand, they agreed to end military intervention against the Bolsheviks and to encourage resumption of trade with Soviet Russia; on the other, they decided to establish a defensive cordon against Bolshevism along Russia's western and southern borders."[117]

With regard to German-Soviet relations, however, what was most important about the Paris Conference was that a peace settlement was made:

"... in the teeth of one of the great powers of Europe and in complete disregard of another. . ."[118]

In a predictive view of the future international political scene, Lenin, on 6th December 1920, offered his insight into what he considered to be three contradictions within the contemporary capitalist world.[119] Two of these predictions, namely, the immediate preparation for war against each other by Japan and the United States, and the hatred of the United States by the rest of the capitalist world were of questionable accuracy at the time at which they were made, but Lenin's third prediction, that of a contradiction between the Allied powers and Germany was, in the wake of the Treaty of Versailles, irrefutable:

"Unable to live under the terms imposed by the Versailles peace, Lenin elaborated, 'Germany must seek an ally against world imperialism. He named the ally on October 2, 1920, in a post-mortem analysis of his egregious blunder in Poland. 'If Poland had been a Soviet country ... the Versailles Peace would have been destroyed, and the entire international system achieved by victories over Germany would have collapsed. France would not then have had a buffer (Poland) separating Germany from Soviet Russia .... The situation was that, given several more days of victorious progress by the Red Army, not only would Warsaw have been taken ... but the Versailles Peace would have been ruined.' This would have indicated to the Germans, he said, 'that in its struggle for survival, the Soviet Republic was the only force in the world that was combating imperialism - and imperialism now means an alliance of France, England and America."[120]

To make an accord with Russia appear both desirable and expedient in German eyes, Lenin offered to them the prospect of a vulnerable France and Britain, and played upon the German feeling of injustice which the Treaty of Versailles had occasioned:

"To make the French and British look less formidable and a German alliance with Russia more alluring, Lenin added that France was 'on the way to bankruptcy' and - equally untrue - even the old *leaders of the British workers 'who formerly opposed the dictatorship of the working class have now come over to our side.'*

Lenin directed his offer of an alliance at Germans nursing the wounds of defeat

...Their opposition to imperialism as embodied in the Versailles peace treaty differed little in intent from communist anti-imperialism. The extreme touch; right meets left."[121]

The grounds of such an offer by Lenin were almost certain to prove attractive to the majority of Germans. To those of a Marxist persuasion Lenin was offering an alliance in opposition to capitalism, whilst to those of a nationalistic persuasion he held out the prospect of Soviet support for their grievance over the treatment which Germany had received at Paris. Whilst such an appeal as that made by Lenin might well have been calculated to unify the German people it had the opposite effect upon Soviet foreign policy with regard to Germany:

" ... Lenin gave Russia two conflicting goals: collaboration with the German army and promotion of a German communist revolution. "[122]

The question of German-Soviet military collaboration in the inter-war period has been dealt with elsewhere in this series of papers [123] and the communist revolution in Germany never occurred despite the promising signs exhibited in the first few days of November 1918.[124] Effectively, the prospect of a communist revolution in Germany had its fate sealed by the Armistice of 11th November 1918 and was certainly a thing of the past by the first national elections to the Reichstag on 6th June 1920.[125]

Yet there was undoubtedly a shared opposition to the major western powers by Germany and Soviet Russia which was eventually to lead to the signing of the Treaty of Rapallo on 16th April 1922. That Treaty comprised five Articles of which three are worthy of particular note as they revealed the preparedness of both signatories to commence relationships anew with old matters of dispute resolved. Article I wiped the slate clean of all governmental and private claims and counterclaims of each party which had arisen in the course of the First World War. Article III provided for the immediate resumption of consular and diplomatic relations between the two countries and Article V was an undertaking that both would work together to alleviate their economic difficulties, whilst declaring, at the same time, a preparedness on the part of the German Government to facilitate the development of economic contacts between the private enterprises in each country.[126] To this extent the Treaty of Rapallo may be seen as an attempt by the two powers most disadvantaged by the provisions of the Treaty of Versailles to circumvent the strictures which it placed upon each of them.

A shared opposition to the Treaty of Versailles was not, however, the only basis for German-Soviet accord:

> "The community of interests created by the similarity of their positions vis-a-vis the Versailles system was reinforced by the fact that the two nations complemented each other in the economic field. Russia had become even more of an agrarian country than before the war. Its pre-war industry lay

in ruins and could only be restored with German assistance. It needed industrial credits and technical assistance and could get them only in Germany ... To Germany, on the other hand, Russia had always been a market for industrial exports."[127]

If a shared opposition to Versailles and complementary economic systems are advanced as reasons for the Treaty of Rapallo and the accord which that both symbolised and heralded between Germany and Soviet Russia, there were other factors which undoubtedly played a part in the developing rapprochement,

> *"In the first place, the German military did not accept defeat and considered the humiliating peace treaty an undeserved stain on the honour of the German army and the German people, a stain to be removed at all costs. Consequently, the German regular army officers did not for a moment seriously accept any of those paragraphs of the Versailles Treaty which forbade the restoration of German military power. They determined on rearmament to rectify, in whatever manner necessary, 'the injustices of the peace settlement.'*

> *A Germany bent on revenge could regain its armed might only with the help of the Soviet Union, which stood outside the Versailles system. For their part, the Communist rulers of Soviet Russia had never given up their idée fixe of a world revolution. They believed that it was necessary for them as quickly as possible to revive industry and build up the Red Army, in order to be ready to support revolution in*

other countries. In backward Russia, military as well as industrial power could most easily be created with the help of German industry, capital and technical assistance. Thus in both Germany and Russia - the two pariahs of the Versailles system - the need for a close partnership was clearly recognised ..."[128]

Clearly both individual and mutual benefit could be derived from German-Soviet accord and Rapallo represented the first formal step along that path.

The Treaty of Rapallo was also significant in that, not only was it an agreement between two nations who felt themselves to have been victims of the major western powers, but also in that it represented the first move taken by Soviet Russia into the post-war international political arena:

"The treaty was most significant as a protest against Versailles. It was an act of friendship by revisionist powers in defiance of the victor nations. Rapallo also deprived the Allies of their most effective weapon against the Communist regime: their ability to isolate her economically and politically. In practical terms, Germany used its good relations with Russia to train an illegal army in the Ukraine and to experiment with new weapons - especially airplanes, which were forbidden to her by Versailles. The Soviets benefited from German aid in building the Red Army into one of the most modern in Europe, along German lines."[129]

As Carr likewise notes,

"The terms of the treaty were unimportant. But its signature was a significant event. It secured for the

Soviet Union its first official recognition by a Great Power; and it was the first overt attempt by Germany to break the ring which the Versailles Powers had drawn around her. The indignation with which this treaty was greeted by the Allied Powers was understandable. But it was the direct consequence of their own policy of treating Germany and the Soviet Union as inferior countries. The two outcasts naturally joined hands; and the Rapallo Treat established friendly relations between them for more than ten years."[130]

But it should not be thought that Rapallo only had implications for Germany and Soviet Russia; it also had important consequences for the western powers, as Kennan notes,

"...Rapallo meant the forfeiture of the collaboration of Germany as a possible partner in a united Western approach to the problem of Russian Communism ... (it) could justly be described as the first great victory for Soviet diplomacy. It successfully split the Western community in its relation to Russia. It drove an entering wedge, on terms favourable to Moscow, into the problem of diplomatic recognition and the resumption of trade relations between Russia and the West."[131]

and in not dissimilar fashion, Fischer holds that,

"Rapallo breached the solid capitalist front against Soviet Russia and strengthened the Bolsheviks' faith in their survival."[132]

References

1   Morris D S, Haigh R H and Peters A R, "Forging the Peace : The Soviet Union and the Paris Peace Conference 1919"

2   Message to President Wilson prepared by the Prime Ministers of Britain, France and Italy meeting at Versailles, 2nd June 1918, and cited in Snyder Louis L "**Historical Documents of World War I**" Van Nostrand. Princeton NJ. 1958 pp 173-4. Authors' emphasis.

3   Collier Basil, "**Barren Victories : Versailles to Suez 1918-1956**" Doubleday & Co. Garden City. NY 1964 p7.

4   ibid p7.

5   An assessment of the military situation confronting the Germans in the summer and autumn of 1918 is to be found in Morris, Haigh and Peters op cit.

6   Letter from Field Marshall Hindenburg to the Imperial Chancellor, Prince Max von Baden, dated 3rd October 1918. Cited in Baden Prince Max von. "**Memoirs of Prince Max of Baden**" Constable & Co, London. 1928, Vol II, p 19.

7   Baden Prince Max von, ibid p23.

8   Collier op cit p11.

9   ibid p12.

10   ibid p22.

11   ibid p24.

12   Snyder op cit pp 177-8.

13   Lansing Robert, **"The Peace Negotiations"** Constable & Co Ltd, London 1921, pp 170-171 & passim. Lansing himself laid down a far more detailed programme than that offered by the Fourteen Points, for this, see pp 171-175.

14   Lipson E. **"Europe 1914-1939"** Adam & Charles Black, London 1957, p 311.

15   These counter-proposals related essentially to specific aspects of the draft treaty and covered matters relating to the League of Nations, territorial questions, German rights and interests outside Germany, the question of reparations, provisions regarding commercial policy, inland navigation, prisoners of war, etc. The complete comments of the German delegation on the conditions of peace contained in the draft treaty are to be found in **"International Conciliation"** No 143, October 1919, pp 1203 and passim.

16   ibid p 1216.

17   ibid p 1220.

18   **"International Conciliation"** American Association for International Conciliation, New York, October 1919, No 143, p 1205 and passim. It is interesting to note Prince Max von Baden's comparison of the treaty with President Wilson's Fourteen Points; see Baden op cit, pp 369-381.

19   **"International Conciliation"** American Association for International Conciliation, New York, November 1919, No 144, p 1353. The

correspondence referred to is the German request to President Wilson of 5th November 1918 for him to arrange an armistice; President Wilson's letter of 23rd October 1918 declaring his willingness to arrange an armistice and containing suggestions for internal political reform in Germany; the German reply of 27th October 1918 to Wilson's communique of 23rd October; Wilson's notification to the German Government of 3rd .November 1918 that the Allies had agreed to peace, with some qualifications, on the basis of the Fourteen Points.

20   **"International Conciliation"** No 143 op cit, p 1208.

21   **"International Conciliation"** No 144 op cit, p 1343 and passim.

22   The territories conceded to Belgium were Moresnet, Eupen and Malmedy.

23   The prebiscite was held in 1935 and resulted in the Saar Basin being re-united with Germany.

24   Part III of Treaty of Versailles.

25   Part IV of Treaty of Versailles. These German colonial possessions were assigned under a mandate from the League of Nations and, therefore, were held in trust and not in ownership by the recipient nations.

26   Grenville J A S **"The Major International Treaties 1914-1973"** Methuen & Co Ltd, London 1974, p 43.

27 A Reparation Commission was established to determine by 1st May 1921 the total of Germany's obligations.

28 Grenville op cit, p 44. The most thorough treatment of the Paris Peace Conference is to be found in Temperley H W V (ed). **"A History of the Peace Conference of Paris"** Vols I-VI published by the joint committee of Henry Frowde, Hodder and Stoughton under the auspices of the Institute for International Affairs, London, 1920. This is an indispensable source for all aspects of the conference.

29 Baker, R Stannard. **"Woodrow Wilson and the World Settlement"** William Heinneman Ltd, London 1923, Vol II, p64.

30 Thompson John N. **"Russia, Bolshevism, and the Versailles Peace"** Princeton University Press, Princeton NJ 1966, p 4.

31 Silverlight John. **"The Victors' Dilemma"** Barrie and Jenkins Ltd, London. 1970, p 6.

32 Allied intervention continued well after the Armistice. For a full account of Allied intervention in Russia see Silverlight ibid.

33 Japan certainly had interests in Asiatic Russia and Siberia; Britain was not lacking in those who were anxious to have a say in the affairs of the Trans-Caspian and Trans-Caucasian regions if for no other reason than to provide a buffer zone between Russia and British India; the French were not without ambitions to have at least economic, if not political, control of the Ukraine and South

Russia; whilst the United States could be counted upon to restrict any possible increase in Japan's sphere of interest in Asia.

34   Thompson John M, op cit p33.

35   Temperley, op cit. Vol VI, pp 311-312.

36   Thompson John M, op cit, p46.

37   ibid p 46.

38   ibid p 46.

39   ibid p 46.

40   ibid p 53.

41   ibid p 51.

42   ibid pp51 -52.

43   ibid p 55.

44   ibid p 57.

45   ibid p 60.

46   ibid p 61.

47   Kennan George F, "**Russia and the West under Lenin and Stalin**" Little Brown & Co, Boston, 1961, p120.

48   ibid pp 123-124.

49   Thompson Charles T. "**The Peace Conference Day By Day**" Brentano's, New York, 1920, pp110-12.

50   Thompson John M, op cit, pp 63-64. For details of the secret treaties referred to see Baker op cit, Vol 1, pp 47-63.

51 For the origins and composition of the Russian Political Conference, see Thomspon John M, ibid, pp 64-78.

52 Thompson Charles T. op cit, pp 116-117.

53 Thompson John M. op cit, p 127.

54 ibid, p128.

55 Mayer Arno J, **"Politics and Diplomacy of Peacemaking"** Weidenfeld and Nicolson, London, 1968, p 430.

56 Thompson John M, op cit, pp 127-128.

57 ibid. pp 119-126.

58 ibid p122.

59 ibid pp 115-116.

60 er op cit, p 439.

61 ibid p 440.

62 Kennan, op cit, p125.

63 ibid p128.

64 Lloyd George David. **"The Truth About. The Peace Treaties"** Victor Gollancz, London 1938. p 324.

65 ibid p327.

66 ibid p368. Authors' emphasis.

67 Kennan, op cit, p129.

68 ibid p129.

69 ibid pp129-130.

70   ibid p130.

71   Lloyd George, op cit, p368.

72   cited ibid, p370. In the event this scheme came to nothing.

73   See Thompson John N. op cit, pp137-139 for details of these further efforts by Churchill.

74   Lloyd George, op cit, p 332

75   Kennan op cit, p125. Bullitt was an attache to the American delegation at the Peace Conference and later was to be the first United States Ambassador to the Soviet Union.

76   ibid, p131. In the event the French were officially notified of Bullitt's mission only two weeks before his return to Paris.

77   Thompson John M. op cit, p152.

78   cited ibid, pp152-53.

79   ibid p154.

80   ibid p154.

81   ibid 163-164.

82   ibid pp168-169. Details of the agenda for the proposed conference, which would not have been subject to revision by either party are to be found in ibid pp 169-170.

83   ibid p240.

84   ibid p239.

85   ibid p243.

86   ibid p247.

87   ibid p162.

88   ibid p155.

89   ibid pp 158-159.

90   Kennan op cit p131. The document referred to is the agreed conditions for a meeting between delegates of the Bolsheviks and the Western Powers and the agenda for proposed conference on neutral territory.

91   ibid p137.

92   ibid p137.

93   The Commission for Relief in Belgium was an American organisation which had enjoyed considerable success in sending food to Belgium during the time it was occupied by the Germans in the First World War. Hoover, a firm anti-interventionist where Russia was concerned, was later to become President of the United States.

94   Kennan, op cit, p138.

95   Thompson John M, op cit, p249.

96   It had been muted in the early part of 1918 and on occasions throughout that year, particularly by the Americans.

97   Nansen, a noted Arctic explorer, had been an active participant in a number of humanitarian organisations both before and during the First. World War.

98   Thompson John M, op cit, pp256-227. The difficulties Nansen experienced in dispatching the message containing the offer of the relief programme to Moscow epitomises the lack of enthusiasm for the plan which existed in the Allied camp. The offer was eventually transmitted by radio from Germany after the British, French and Dutch had declined to do so.

99   Kennan, op cit, p140.

100   ibid p 141.

101   Thompson John N, op cit, p260.

102   Kennan, op cit, p142.

103   Mayer, op cit, pp485-487.

104   Thompson John N, op cit, p265.

105   ibid. p266.

106   ibid p267.

107   ibid p278, p282, p292.

108   Mayer, op cit, p824.

109   ibid p824.

110   ibid p824.

111   Britain, France, Italy, Japan and the United States.

112   Mayer op cit p825.

113   ibid p825.

114   ibid p825.

115   Thompson John N, op cit p34.6.

116 ibid p346.

117 ibid p346.

118 Baker Ray Stannard, cited in Thompson John N, ibid p 397.

119 Fischer Louis **"Russia's Road from Peace to War"** Harper and Row, New York 1969, p50.

120 ibid pp 50-51.

121 ibid p 51.

122 ibid p 80.

123 Peters A R, Haigh R H and Morris D S, "Soldiers Against Versailles : The Reichswehr and the Red Army 1921-1933"

124 Especially the events of 4th-9th November 1918. See Baden Prince Max von, op cit, Chs XI - XIV.

125 Fischer, op cit p89. At these elections the Social Democrats received 6,104,000 votes and became the majority party with 102 seats, The Independent Social Democrats polled 5,046,800 votes and took 84 seats, whilst the Communists captured but 589,000 votes and 2 seats.

126 The text of the treaty can be found in Grenville J A S, op cit pp139-140.

127 Abramovitch Raphael R. **"The Soviet Revolution 1917-1939"** George Allen and Unwin Ltd, London 1962, p244.

128 ibid pp244-245.

129 Sumler David E. "A History of Europe in the 20th Century" The Dorsey Press, Homewood I11, 1973, p 105.

130 Carr E H, "**International Relations Between the Two World Wars (1919-1939)**"Macmillan & Co Ltd, London, 1959, p75.

131 Kennan, op cit, p222.

132 Fischer, op cit, p 104.

Chapter Five

Russo-German Military Collaboration 1921-1923

On December 11, 1918 exactly one month after the conclusion of the armistice, the German armed forces returning from the frontlines marched triumphantly through the streets of Berlin. Upon their assembly at the Brandenburger Tor, Friedrich Ebert, Chancellor of the Provisional Government following the resignation of the Imperial regime, received the troops with a statement that declared:

> "I salute you, who return unvanquished from the field of battle[1]"

Yet within eight months, with the signing of the Treaty of Versailles, the German armed forces appeared anything but unvanquished.[2] The powerful military machine so carefully groomed by von Falkenhayn, Hindenburg and Ludendorff had been technically reduced to the strength and status of a domestic police force. The core of the Prussian military tradition, which was developed through the military academies and cadet schools and finally concentrated in the institution of the General Staff, was to be completely dismantled.[3]

Three out of every four officers would have to be dismissed to conform with the demand that the German army be reduced to a maximum strength of one hundred thousand men.[4] The army was to be denied access to all major offensive weapons such as submarines, tanks and aeroplanes, while the import of war materials was expressly prohibited. The German armament industry was to be largely turned over to other usages, while the remnants were to be subject to close Allied scrutiny and regulation. Finally, the demilitarisation of the Rhineland seemed to effectively nullify Germany's ability to defend its western frontiers against the overwhelming military superiority that the French army possessed as a result of the Versailles terms.[5]

The position of the German armed forces in society had been built on the acceptance of the Prussian Junker tradition in both the political and military spheres of the German state. In 1919 this bond appeared to have been irrevocably severed with the abdication of the Kaiser and the establishment of a Republican form of Government which was based essentially on politicians drawn from the left of the political spectrum. The Kapp Putsch staged in March 1920 outwardly seemed to represent a desperate attempt by right wing militarist and monarchist elements to reassert their predominence.[6] The fact that the Putsch was effectively thwarted by organised labour enforcing a General Strike while the German armed forces declined to either support or suppress the insurrection seemed to symbolise the comparative decline of right wing influence within the German state. In this context the decision of the German Army to adopt a role of political neutrality was of central importance.[7] In the latter years of the war the General Staff had enjoyed a position of almost unparalleled political authority under the leadership of Hindenburg and Ludendorff.[8] The fact that the Reichswehr in 1919 elected to remain politically impartial appeared to confirm the suspicion that the Treaty of Versailles had rendered the German Army both politically and militarily impotent.[9]

Despite the physical and political restrictions imposed in 1919 the German army emerged from the dark days of the immediate post Versailles period to become within two decades one of the most effective fighting forces on the European continent. The basis of this achievement can be traced largely to the work of one man, General Hans von Seeckt. In both lineage and outward appearance Seeckt appeared to represent the personification of the Prussian military tradition.[10] He had been appointed to the General Staff Corps at the exceptionally early age of thirty-three and during the war had acquitted himself well as Chief of Staff to Mackensen's 11th Army on the eastern front and later as Chief of the Turkish General Staff. Recognised as one of the most incisive brains within the German General Staff, Seeckt was seconded to the Paris Peace Conference as senior military adviser to the German delegation. At Paris he had been surprised at the severity of the disarmament clauses imposed by the Allies but, while many of his contemporaries advocated rejection of the terms and the overthrow of any German government that accepted them, Seeckt appreciated the realities of the situation.[12] Following his appointment as Deputy Chief of Staff and, later Chief of the Army High Command, he accepted the post of Chairman of the

Preparatory Commission on the Peace Army and quietly undertook to rebuild he Reichswehr.[13]

It had been Seeckt in March 1920 who had declined to involve his troops in the Kapp Putsch.[14] In reply to a request by the Minister of Defence to dispatch troops to disarm General Walter Luttwitz's Freikorps, Seeckt replied:

"Troops do not fire on troops. Do you perhaps intend, Herr Minister, that a battle be fought before the Brandenburg Gate between troops who have fought side by side against the common enemy."[15]

It was considered that as Seeckt had not committed his forces to the support of the putsch he was therefore a traitor and hireling of the Socialist government. However, to adopt. such a stance was to render Seeckt a great disservice.[16] His ultimate loyalty to the Prussian military tradition, which his family had served for generations, and his dedication to the role of the monarchy could never be doubted yet he was far more pragmatic in his outlook than were many of his fellow officers.[17] The British Ambassador to Berlin, Viscount O'Abernon concluded that Seeckt had:

"...a broader outlook than is expected in so tight a uniform, a wider outlook than seems appropriate to so precise, so correct, so neat an exterior"[18]

Alistair Horne also took up this theme:

"His monocle and hard features, making him seem like a traditional, rigid Prussian Junker, in fact concealed a remarkable elasticity and breadth of vision"[19]

The tenor of Seeckt's concept of the role of the new Reichswehr was established in his first Order of the Day issued on April 18, 1920:

"This is a crucial hour for the officer corps of the new Reichswehr. Its behaviour in the immediate future will determine whether the officer corps will retain the leadership in the new army"[20]

"The old spirit of silent self-effacing devotion in the service of the Army, which in this moment more full of danger than ever before, does not permit anyone to withhold his services for the common weal"[21]

"We do not inquire into the political life of individuals, but must assume of everyone who remains in the Army, that he loyally respects his oath and accepts of his own free will and as an honourable soldier, the constitution of the Reich."[22]

In the period immediately following the Kapp Putsch, when the political parties of the left were baying for a dramatic purging, if not a complete dismantlement of the regular army, this statement appeared to represent a concession to the opponents of the Reishswehr.[23] However, in essence, it incorporated the basis of Seeckt's philosophy. His loyalty lay not with the Provisional government, or even the Kaiser, but with the German nation and the concept of the Reich.[24]

"The Reich! There is something supernatural in this word. It embraces far more and connotes something other than the conception of a State. It does not stand for the State institutions of today."

"It is an organic living entity subject to the laws of evolution"[25]

Within this framework Seeckt saw the role of the armed forces as one of maintaining this tradition:

"The Army should become a State within the State, but it should be merged in the State through service; in fact it should itself become the purest image of the State."[26]

Seeckt, therefore, saw his primary duty as the maintenance of the traditions and spirit of the German Army as the cornerstone of the Reich. Yet the army had been dealt grievous blows by both the war and the subsequent peace settlement. It was still under severe attack from left wing political elements and obviously needed a period of recuperation and reorganisation.[27] While this was being undertaken Seeckt saw nothing incongruous in pledging the support of the armed forces to the Weimar Republic and furthermore making it clear that he would not permit the army to interfere in the sphere of domestic politics.[28] In the pursuit of political stability the Reichswehr and the Weimar Republic shared a common goal and, therefore, Seeckt firmly repressed uprisings of both left and right wing extremists that threatened this stability during the early years of the Republic.[29] The bond was cemented by the fact that the Weimar Republic, fearful of extremist opposition from both ends of the political spectrum, appreciated the value of the pillar of support offered by the Reichswehr.

With this tacit alliance established, Seeckt was able to devote his full attention to the rebuilding of the German army. At the Spa Conference of July 1920 the limitation of the Reichswehr to 100,000 men had been confirmed.[31] Within this limit Seeckt set out to completely rebuild and reorganise the Reichswehr as the future nucleus of the German army, once the Versailles restrictions had been lifted or circumvented. To this end, although the force was technically limited to 4,000 officers at any one time, up to 40,000 men were trained as non-commissioned officers and were equipped to form the basis of a greatly expanded officer corps. Furthermore, the restriction on the number of recruits permitted the setting of high intellectual and physical standards.[32] All army equipment was effectively standardised and illicit plans established for the mobilisation of manpower and the economy in time of war.[33] As Alistair Horne noted:

> *"The result was a remarkably professional, technically efficient force in miniature."*[34]

In terms of strategy, Seeckt had served extensively on the eastern front and had masterminded the dramatic breakthrough at Gorlice in May 1915. Unlike many of his contemporaries who had become preoccupied with defensive strategy Seeckt remained a firm advocate of offensive tactics.[35] He insisted that the lesson of the war had been that only mobility and flexibility in the deployment of the army could produce a decisive victory. As Churchill later recorded, Seeckt concluded:

> *"... that false doctrines, springing from personal experiences of the Great War, should be avoided. All the lessons of that war were thoroughly and systematically studied. New principles of training and instructional courses of all kinds were*

introduced. All the existing manuals were rewritten."[36]

The core of this strategy was to be based on the harnessing of modern technology and the utilisation of motorised armoured vehicles supported by self propelled guns, aircraft and infantry."[37] Seeckt unashamedly developed his tactics along the lines being established by the British military strategists Liddell Hart and J F C Fuller.[38] As General Heinz Guderian later testified Seeckt established the ground work for a unique form of offensive warfare based on the deployment of largescale motorised forces using surprise and speed to penetrate deeply through the enemy lines.[39]

However, from the outset the Versailles terms denied the Reichswehr the possession of largescale forces, tanks or airplanes. The first of these problems Seeckt originally overcame by the training of troops within the police force and also by the creation of thinly disguised auxiliary military units such as the Arbeits-Kommandos which were later associated with the Black Reichswehr.[40] Furthermore within the Ministry of Defence the framework of the General Staff (Truppenant) was covertly reconstituted. Seeckt did not entertain any doubts that the subtle bending and, at times, outright infringement of the Versailles terms was both justified and essential.[41] Yet in both technical and strategic terms there were limits to what Seeckt could achieve within the frontiers of Weimar Germany. Although at least at one stage during the war Seeckt had actively considered the possibility of a peace settlement with the western powers at the expense of Russia,[42] he had never forcibly subscribed to the

Greater German school of thought, which had been at its zenith at the time of the Treaty of Brest-Litovsk with the advocation of a firm Austro-German alliance directed against Russia.[43] Following the conclusion of the Treaty of Versailles, Seeckt reviewed the political and military advantages of an understanding with Bolshevik Russia:

> *"The re-establishment of a broad common frontier between Russia and. Germany is the precondition of the regaining of strength of both countries."*[44]

> *"The Russian dangers rest in the area of ideas therefore, although Germany does not subscribe to the Bolshevik form of Government, she must look upon Russia as two separate things. That is, political Russia for German benefit and Soviet Russia to be treated as a danger. The only trouble in making this distinction is that in politics the Russians will not leave out their Bolshevism, for Russia's political goal is the organisation of the Slavic lands into one large Soviet. However, this does not have to disturb Germany for it would solve the problem of our Polish enemy and, instead of putting Russia on the offensive, it would place her on the defensive as a potential bulwark against the yellow races to her east. So it can be seen that the interests of Germany and Russia are not in conflict."*[45]

Despite the ideological gulf between the two regimes Seeckt considered that on several grounds the Treaty of Versailles had created areas of mutual interest for Bolshevik Russia and Germany. Primarily this interest was based on their common distrust and hatred of the Polish state created in 1919 which had been reconstituted with provinces taken essentially from Germany and Russia. Berlin and Moscow shared the common conviction that Poland represented a

> *potential threat to their national security that was unacceptable.*[46] *In September 1922 Seeckt reiterated this opinion:*

> *"Poland's existence is intolerable, incompatible with the survival of Germany. It must disappear and it will disappear through its own internal weakness and through Russia - with our assistance."*[47]

Seeckt appreciated that for the present time the threat of French retaliation effectively eliminated the possibility of German forces assisting the Bolsheviks in the destruction of the Polish state. However, he was anxious to explore the possibility of a tacit alliance being established in the field of military reorganisation and training. The Reichswehr had need of secret foreign facilities to train soldiers and manufacture forbidden war materials while the Bolsheviks urgently required the skills of western economic and military expertise to rebuild the Russian war machine.[48]

Major Fritz Tschunke, who was later to play a central role in the creation of military links between Germany and Soviet Russia, claimed that Seeckt urged the German forces to open links with the Red Army during the Baltic campaign in 1919.[49] However, by May 1919 it was increasingly apparent that the Freikorps in the Baltic states, led by General von der Goltz, were intent on overthrowing the Bolshevik government in Moscow before marching west to restore the monarchy in Berlin.[50] Although Seeckt may have sympathised with their nationalist aspirations he also appreciated that their activities represented an increasing source of irritation in relations with Soviet Russia on the one hand and Britain and France on the other. He was therefore not unhappy to see the Baltic operation wound up in the autumn of 1919.[51]

Throughout 1919 informal contacts were tentatively established between Moscow and Berlin using the agency of the Commission for the Repatriation of War Prisoners.[52] Furthermore, several high ranking military officers held discussions with the Bolshevik emissary, Karl Radek, who had been imprisoned in Berlin in January 1919,[53] while Enver Bey, the former Turkish Minister for War, whom Seeckt had assisted in his journey to Russia, pressed the German cause in Moscow.[54]The possibility of a Russo-German understanding appeared to have been given further impetus by the Bolshevik victories in Poland in the first half of 1920. Despite the apprehension felt by many of the Weimar politicians, Seeckt enthusiastically welcomed the prospect of a Bolshevik victory in Poland. He considered that a Soviet victory would remove the Polish threat to Germany's eastern frontier and would also force the western powers to rearm Germany in order to form a bulwark against the further dissemination of Bolshevism.[55] In this appreciation of the situation Seeckt found a valuable and powerful ally in Baron Ago von Maltzan, Head of the East European section of the Foreign Ministry. Until Maltzan was transferred to Washington in 1923 he consistently supported Seeckt in the quest for an informal alliance with Soviet Russia.[56]

Ironically, however, it was the defeat of the Red Army at Warsaw in August 1920 that produced the first major initiative in Russo-German military relations. Although Radek in Berlin had talked enthusiastically of the possibility of an alliance with Germany it would seem that the mood in Moscow was almost unanimously against any such alignment. Lenin and the Bolshevik hierarchy saw the successful conclusion of the Civil War and the dramatic westward advance of the Red Army through Poland as heralding the imminent declaration of the European proletarian revolution.[57] Within this framework any future alliances would be with the German working classes and not with the incumbent capitalist governments.[58] However the reversal of military fortunes in Poland, which resulted in the Treaty of Riga in March 1921, coupled with the failure of the Communist uprising in Germany in the same month forced Lenin to reappraise his tactics.[59] An indication of this reorientation of attitudes had been noted in a letter to Seeckt from Enver Bey in August 1920:

> "Yesterday (ie on 25 August) I had a talk with Sklanski (Deputy People's Commissar for War), the deputy and right hand man of Trotsky... A party here, which has real power and to which -Trotsky too belongs is in favour of a rapprochement with Germany. Sklanski said: this party would be willing to recognise the old German frontier of 1914. And they see only one way out of the world's chaos: co-operation with Germany and Turkey"[60]

This represented the first positive indication from Moscow that the Bolsheviks were prepared to publicly concede that the European revolution was not imminent and that a working relationship would have to be established with the capitalist regimes to permit the rebuilding of the Russian economy while the conditions for revolution matured.[61] The dilemma within the Bolshevik hierarchy was reflected by the increasing division of opinion between the President of the Comintern, Zinoviev, who insisted that ideologically and practically it was not possible to work with the capitalist states and the Commissar for Foreign Affairs, Chicherin, who favoured a more pragmatic approach to the problem of economic relations with the west.[62] In December 1920 Lenin appeared to be moving towards Chicherin's stance when he pointed out that Germany, although a capitalist state, had effectively been made an outcast by the Treaty of Versailles. In such circumstances it should be possible for Russia to exploit this situation to its own advantage.[63] Lenin concluded that:

> "... this country bound by the Versailles Treaty, finds itself in circumstances that make its existence impossible. And in such a position Germany is naturally pushed into alliance with Russia."[64]

In a similar vein Lenin also noted:

> "I am not fond of the Germans by any means but at the present time it is more advantageous to use them than to challenge them. An independent Poland is very dangerous to Soviet Russia: it is an evil which, however, at the present time has also its redeeming features; for while it exists, we may safely count on Germany, because the Germans hate Poland and will at any time make common cause with us on order to strangle Poland .... Everything teaches us to look

upon Germany as our most reliable ally. Germany wants revenge, and we want revolution. For the moment our aims are the same."[65]

Following the suppression of the German Communist uprising Lenin conceded:

"It is plain at a glance that, after the conclusion of the peace, however bad that was, we did not succeed in provoking a revolution in the capitalist countries.... What is essential now is a fundamental preparation of the revolution, and a study of its concrete development in the principal capitalist countries"[66]

With this admission that there would have to be a "breathing space" and a form of detente with the capitalist nations before the final revolutionary assault the path was cleared for the opening of limited relations with the western powers where they were of positive benefit to Soviet Russia.[67]

The most immediate problem lay in the field of economic affairs with the need to resuscitate the war ravaged Soviet economy. In this area the potential benefits to be derived from western technology and organisation in the rebuilding of Russian industry were self evident. In March 1921 Lenin launched the New Economic Policy and in the same month confirmed the intention to establish a commercial rapprochement with the west with the negotiation of the Anglo-Russian Trade Agreement.[68]

When in May 1921 negotiations were opened in Berlin for a similar Russo-German Commercial Agreement, the Reichswehr was ready to grasp the opportunity to open direct links with Moscow. In anticipation of such a situation arising Seeckt had created a clandestine unit within the Ministry of Defence called Sondergruppe R, specifically to conduct military negotiations with their Bolshevik counterparts.[69] Seeckt was aware that following the conclusion of the Russo-Polish War Lenin had formally applied to the German Ministry of Defence for aid in the reconstruction of the Soviet armed forces. He was also aware that the Soviets were interested in acquiring technical aid in the rebuilding of their industrial strength. Therefore, initially, the role of Sondergruppe R was to foster relations between German industry and the various semi-official Soviet representatives in Berlin. As a result of this work a delegation from Sondergruppe R was invited to visit the Soviet Union in the spring of 1921 to assess the extent of technical aid that would be required to reconstruct the military sector of the Soviet economy.[70] The delegation consisted of Major Fritz Tschunke, who was later to supervise the co-ordination of the production of German war materials in Russia, Major Oskar Ritter von Niedermayer, whose responsibility was to lie in the promotion of direct links between the respective armed forces, and a former military attaché to Russia, Lieutenant Schubert.[71] Their report concluded that the devastation of the Russian industrial machine was so vast that it would be an impossible task to provide a comprehensive restoration scheme.[72] However, they did see the potential for limited aid on specific schemes to produce munitions and aircraft. On the basis of this report Radek and Leonid Krassin, the Soviet Commissar for Foreign Trade, held discussions with Major Kurt von Schleicher and General Paul von Hasse in Berlin in September 1921 where the basis of German military and economic aid to the Soviet Union was established.[73] Tschunke summarised the outcome of these negotiations:

> "The result of our work, which was conducted with all caution both at home and abroad for reasons self evident, was the establishment of "Gesellschaft zur Foerderung gewerblicher Unter nehmungen (Gefu)" with offices both in Berlin and Moscow. Directions were given me to confide my order or needs of considerable capital to the Reichsregierung (Wirth and Maltzan)"[74]

Tschunke outlined Gefu's terms of reference:

1) Concessions agreement with the Junkers Aircraft Works for the purpose of the Russian government to manufacture metal airplane parts, airplanes and motors at the Fili factory near Moscow.

2) Establishment of the German-Russian joint stock company Bersol near Samara to build a chemical factory to make poison gas.

3) The manufacture for us of artillery ammunition with German technical assistance.[75]

Agreement was also reached on the establishment of direct links between the Reichswehr and the Red Army with Soviet officers being invited to attend Staff officer training courses in Berlin and also co-operating in the creation of tank and air training schools in Russia for the Reichswehr. Niedermayer was to set up an independent military centre in Moscow to administer these military connections.[76]

Although Chicherin, the Soviet Commissar for Foreign Affairs, confirmed that German officers were at

work in Russia as early as April 1922[77] the final details
of the economic links to be established between German
and Russian industry were not finalised until late into
the summer of 1922.[78] Sondergruppe R played a major
role in the creation of these arrangements by assuring
the major Ruhr industrialists representing Krupps and
Junkers that there would not be any political risks and
that they would be provided with extensive financial
assistance in their operations.[79] For the initial year of
the programme the basis of this assistance was to be
founded on seventy five million marks provided by the
Ministry of Finance.[80] As the German Chancellor, Josef
Wirth, also held the post of Minister of Finance, it
would appear that the Reichswehr programme was
tacitly supported by the higher echelons of the German
Government. Gustav Hilger noted that Wirth when
questioned about Gefu's activities before the Foreign
Affairs Committee of the Reichsteig in 1927:

> "... admitted,...., that the deals had not been made by
> the War Ministry without the Cabinet's knowledge,
> but that he, Wirth, had, "stood at the very cradle of
> relations with Russia," together with General von
> Seeckt. He vigorously came out in favour of
> Ostpolitik, holding that in 1922 and 1923 it had
> been the greatest achievement of German foreign
> policy."[81]

It would seem that French intransigence over the
reparations issue had significantly reduced Wirth's faith
in a policy of co-operation with Britain and France.[82]
The temptation to look eastwards to the Soviet Union as
a potential counterbalance to French influence was
reflected not only in the military sphere but also in the

diplomatic field with the conclusion of the Treaty of Rapallo in April 1922.

At Rapallo, Germany and the Soviet Union agreed to resume full diplomatic and commercial relations. Despite the apprehension felt in many circles concerning the Anglo-French reaction to the treaty, Seeckt greeted it openly as the first step towards restoring German independence and prestige within Europe. Although Seeckt would have preferred to have taken the treaty one step further with a Russo-German pact of mutual assistance against Poland, he was satisfied that the mere existence of a formal Russo-German treaty, with or without a secret military annex, would deter Poland from any precipitate action.[83] Yet, in essence, there was no need for a formal military arrangement for through the work of Sondergruppe R extensive links were being engineered between the Reichswehr and the Red Army.

However, in one respect the terms of the Treaty of Rapallo presented an immediate problem for Seeckt. With the formal renewal of full diplomatic relations it was considered that the bond between the two nations should be consolidated by the seconding of a senior German diplomat to the Moscow Embassy. For this post the Foreign Minister, Rathenau, had proposed Count Brockdorff-Rantzau who had led the German delegation at the Paris Peace Conference.[84] Rantzau was initially reluctant to accept the task for, although he appreciated the benefits to be derived from the Soviet alliance, he also saw very clearly that it would be unpopular with Britain and France and drive them even closer together at a time when German policy should seek to divide the former entente powers and hence reduce French power and influence.[85] In August 1922 Rantzau expressed his fears to Wirth:

"Any appearance of a military alliance on our part with the East would have the most detrimental effect on our relations with the West"

"A German policy orientated exclusively towards the East would at the present moment be not only precipitate and dangerous but without prospect and, therefore, a mistake."[86]

Seeckt, who considered that Rantzau had betrayed the German armed forces at Versailles and had disagreed vehemently with the strategy adopted by Rantzau at the conference, was quick to respond to criticism of the Russo-German alignment.[87] He pointed out that the relationship could only strengthen Germany's hand in dealing with France and Poland:

"We want two things. Firstly a strong Russia, economically, politically, and therefore militarily and thus indirectly a stronger Germany in as far as we would be strengthening a possible ally. We also want, cautiously and tentatively at first, a direct increase of strength for ourselves by helping to build up in Russia an armaments industry which in case of need would be of use to us."[88]

In a direct attack on Rantzau, Seeckt noted:

"... he who sees in the Treaty of Rapallo mainly a political blunder, though perhaps fit to work in another place, would seem to be unfit for the post of German representative in Moscow."[89]

Seeckt also suspected that Rantzau would want to assume control of the Russo German military dialogue:

"In all these measures still largely in the initial phase, participation, and even official recognition by the German Government would be absolutely out of the question. The detailed negotiations could only be conducted by military authorities. It should be taken for granted that the latter make no agreements binding on the Reich without the knowledge of the political authorities. As long as the German Government do not conduct official negotiations, the German Embassy in Moscow is not the proper place in which to negotiate."[90]

However, Seeckt's fears seemed to be largely groundless. Rantzau, upon taking up his post in Moscow, worked tirelessly to improve relations with the Soviet Union[91] and it appeared that the Reichswehr had preserved its independence from the Foreign Ministry when, in November 1922 Dr Gessler, the Minister for Defence, confirmed that all aspects of military policy towards the Soviet Union were to be the responsibility of the Chief of the General Staff (Truppenant)[92]. During 1923, Rantzau continually fought to reverse this latter decision but with little success. He was particularly bitter than the military were allowed to establish their own headquarters in Moscow and therefore exclude the Embassy and Foreign Ministry from their negotiations.[93] In February 1923 following the visit of the Chief of the General Staff, General Otto Hasse, to Moscow, Rantzau wrote to the German Foreign Minister:

"As far as I can see the military are again conducting their arbitrary policy. You know what I want! In the final analysis I have the same aim as the military. But I do not want to have the direction of things taken out of my hands and to have my policy upset."[94]

The ambassador was particularly disturbed by Hasse's openly stated conviction that a war of liberation would be launched in the west within five years.[95] Rantzau also bombarded the Foreign Ministry with reports that the military authorities were entering into agreements that involved the transfer of vast sums of money to Russia without adequate conditions for any form of a proportionate return, either in terms of a military guarantee against Poland or an exclusive economic concession in the Soviet armament industry.[96] The ambassador was convinced that both of the above could be achieved:

"... since in the first place Russia needs us for the reconstruction of her armaments industry, and needs us urgently, because she can find no other power for that purpose; and in the second place, since a successful attack by Poland against Germany, strengthening Poland, would be so dangerous to Russia that she will have a vital interest in preventing such a development."[97]

Partially as a result of Rantzau's protests in the summer of 1923 the German Chancellor, Wilhelm Cuno, transferred the negotiations from Moscow to Berlin[98] and gained assurances from the Russian representative, Rozengolts, concerning aid in any future conflict with Poland and the exclusive rights of German industry to assist and draw upon Soviet armament production.[99] Furthermore, the Reichswehr was instructed to place the overall control of their Moscow headquarters under the administration of the Moscow Embassy. Despite these measures Rantzau continued to voice his concern at the activities of the military in the Soviet Union. In February 1924 the ambassador reported:

> *"I urgently recommend not to spend a penny of German money for war materials in Russia, to limit all orders to a minimum and to use the credits granted by the Reich to support German industries in Russia, not for military purposes, but industries that indirectly serve re-armament."*[100]

Even Niedermayer conceded that:

> *"The sad part is that some gentlemen have acted from motives of personal ambition and in an attempt to conclude treaties at all cost, have committed themselves to the Russians in the most irresponsible way."*[101]

It would seem, therefore, that Rantzau was correct in concluding that the Reichswehr had failed to observe the undertaking outlined by Seeckt in October 1922 and that agreements had been made with the Soviet authorities without the knowledge of the German Foreign Ministry. However, the ambassador was also forced to concede that any attempt to cancel or scale down these arrangements would have severely strained the Russo- German relationship.[102] By 1925 the production of munitions, airplanes and poison gases by the German firms of Krupps, Junkers and Stolzenberg was underway at plants within the Soviet Union.[103]

Furthermore, direct military links had been established between the Reichswehr and the Red Army. Red Army officers attended German manoeuvres and staff officer training courses in Berlin. In return, the Russians provided the Reichswehr with training facilities for tanks, aircraft and chemical warfare at various bases within the Soviet Union. These facilities were the direct responsibility of the Reichswehr headquarters in Moscow which supervised the establishment of the bases and the transport of personnel.[104] The airfields at Smolensk and, after 1923,: at Lipetsk were of particular significance in allowing the Reichswehr to circumvent the restrictions on the maintenance of a German Air Force.

When the airforce was formally disbanded, in line with the disarmament agreement, one hundred and eighty flying officers were transferred to the army. Using the Lipetsk facilities, Fokker D13 aircraft bought in Holland and this small group of aviators the Reichswehr was able to develop the nucleus of a modern airforce fully trained in combat techniques. Furthermore, between 1925 and 1933, approximately one hundred and twenty pilots received their basic training at Lipetsk.[105] The tank training facilities at Kazan were not fully operational until 1925. However, between 1925 and 1933, in a period when tank crews in Germany were forced to practise with dummy canvas models, the base at Kazan, using tanks procured from Britain, Sweden and also illicitly from Germany, provided an invaluable testing ground for the development of the revolutionary Panzer tactics pioneered by Seeckt.[106]

"The establishment of these facilities was undertaken in the 1923-24 period at a time when Seeckt's personal prestige and influence within Germany was at its zenith. However the election of Hindenburg as President of the German Reich in April 1925 marked a shift in the relationship between the Reichswehr and the German government. With the installation of the veteran military leader in the post of President, Seeckt was no longer the sole focus of Reichswehr loyalty. Furthermore, Hindenburg insisted that all military decisions were to be ultimately subject to his personal approval.[107] It seemed that the inevitable reduction in Seeckt's political influence would lead to a clash between Germany's two leading military figures. Yet the expected confrontation never actually materialised. When in the autumn of 1926, Seeckt ill-advisedly permitted the eldest son of the Crown Prince to attend the Reichswehr manoeuvres, neither Hindenburg, as Reich President and Commander-in-Chief of the Armed Forces, Stresemann or Gessler attempted to defend the Chief of the Army High Command during the subsequent uproar in the Reichstag and the national press. Seeckt appreciated the weakness of his position and bowed to the inevitable by tendering his resignation in October 1926.[108]

The sudden removal of the guiding hand from the Russo-German military relationship was also accompanied by two further events that were to produce significant reassessment of the links established during Seeckt's tenure of office. As Rantzau had continually pointed out, the economic activities of the Reichswehr within Russia had been run with the ultimate goal of promoting military co-operation and the production of war materials prohibited within Germany rather than on a purely economic basis in terms of covering the costs of production.[109] By 1926, GEFU was in serious financial difficulties resulting from the rapid inflation of the German mark and the government's reluctance to allocate further funds to the Russian programme. This reluctance was no doubt based on the fact that, except for the receipt of 300,000 artillery grenades, the tangible returns from investment in the Soviet Union had been negligible compared to the extent f the funds allocated to the Reichswehr.[110] Major Tschunke attempted to defend GEFU by claiming that problems had been encountered with the Soviet labour laws and the acquisition of raw materials but could not prevent the firm going into liquidation.[111] GEFU was eventually replaced by Wirkschaftskontor GmbH which was also funded by the Ministry of Defence and effectively took over GEFU's former responsibilities. However, the finance laced at its disposal was severely limited and when further subsidisation was not forthcoming the decision was taken to close the aircraft factory at Fili and the poison gas plant at Trotsk."[112]

The closure of the Fili factory produced unexpected and extensive repercussions in that the Junkers firm, when refused compensation from the German government for its losses in the Soviet Union, passed a detailed memorandum outlining German economic activity in the Soviet Union to each member of the

Reichstag.[113] This document subsequently formed the basis of an article in the Manchester Guardian on December 3, 1926 and a public attack on the German government by Philip Scheidemann, a Social Democrat representative in the Reichstag, on December 16, 1926. Scheidemann demanded the resignation of the Minister of Defence and the abrogation of the illicit military and economic relations between Germany and the Soviet Union. Furthermore, he proposed that a close scrutiny be maintained on the activities of senior Reichswehr personnel and the financing of Reichswehr operations.[114]

The revelations produced the fall of the German government following a vote of no confidence but did not result in the international backlash that might have been anticipated.[115] This can only be explained by reference to two factors. Firstly, it would appear that both Britain and France were aware that covert military links had been forged between the Soviet Union and Germany. Secondly, they had chosen not to expose these links or make extensive political capital out of the Scheidemann revelations because of the fear that it would impair the process of improving relations with Germany. The western powers saw Germany as playing a central role in the containment of Bolshevism and the maintenance of European stability. Therefore, to castigate Germany in December 1926 appeared to threaten the tenuous links established by the Treaty of Locarno in 1925.[116]

The reorientation of German foreign policy towards a mood of co-operation with Britain and France had been largely engineered by Gustav Stresemann. Stresemann was, above all, pragmatic in his assessment of European politics. He considered that the limitations imposed by the Treaty of Versailles were far more likely to be lifted by conciliation and co-operation with the western powers than by any form of hostile and antagonistic policy based on an alliance with the Soviet Union.[117] This shift in stance had been indicated in 1923 when Maltzan, the main protagonist of an eastern policy within the Foreign Ministry, had been transferred to the Washington Embassy and it had been apparently confirmed in 1925 with the conclusion of the Treaty of Locarno.[118] However, Stresemann's ultimate goal was the resurrection of German power and prestige within Europe. In this context, despite his later protestations, he was certainly aware of and approved the military links with the Soviet Union.[119] Stresemann appreciated the need to maintain a modern and efficient army but at the same time he would not tolerate measures that threatened Germany's relations with the western powers. Therefore, to prevent the possibility of a repetition of the Scheidemann revelations, the Foreign Minister insisted that the Russian operations be scaled down and security increased. Furthermore, he dismissed the suggestion that a formal Russo-German military alliance directed specifically against Poland should be established on the grounds that it would create open hostility and suspicion in France and Britain.[120]

It seemed, therefore, inevitable that with the removal of Seeckt, the role of the Reichswehr in the Soviet Union would be considerably reduced. Seeckt's biographer, Rabenau, concluded:

> "During the following period this naturally forced the army to take precautions to cover up and cut

down. And as the authority of Seeckt's personality disappeared much that he had achieved could no longer be maintained."[121]

However, General Kurt von Hammerstein-Equard, Chief of the Army Command from 1930 until 1934, replied to Rabenau by stating:

*"This is incorrect. Seeckt's Russian policy was continued **without** change after his esignation."[122]*

Gustav Hilger, who was attached to the German Embassy in Moscow throughout the 1920's, concluded that the Reichswehr never considered cutting their links with the Red Army.[123] Indeed so great was the fear that the Soviet Union would look to France for military assistance the Reichswehr was prepared to defy any instructions to break ties with the Soviet Union. However, the situation did not arise as Hilger testified:

"All concerned, from Stresemann on down, were resolved not only to continue as before with military co-operation, but to intensify it, though with the greatest caution."[124]

To explain this statement it is important to draw a distinction between economic and military links with the Soviet Union. Prior to 1926 the distinction between the two categories had been deliberately blurred and the Reichswehr had been active in both areas often using the lure of economic assistance to cement relations between the Soviet Union and Germany. As a consequence of the Scheidemann revelations and the collapse of GEFU it was decided that economic links with the Soviet Union were to be scaled down and put on a sound economic footing.[125] The criterion determining investment was to be the direct material benefit to Germany that would be produced. However, the Reichswehr was not unduly sorry to see the Junkers and Bersol factories liquidated during this period. The removal of restrictions on the manufacture of grenades within Germany had partially reduced the need to establish armament factories abroad. Furthermore, the giant Krupps concern had become adept at disguising its illegal preparations for re-armament. Based on the secret Research Department for Arms Production, Krupps were able to commence the large scale production of tanks less than a year after the withdrawal of the Allied Control Commission in 1927.[126] German companies had also gained effective control over several major foreign armament firms. By 1925 the Swedish firm Bofors, which produced heavy guns, anti-aircraft guns and tanks, was controlled by Krupps of Essen,[127] while the German Navy had indirectly established holding companies in Spain and Holland that were engaged in the construction of submarines and torpedoes.[128]

With the expansion of the armament production facilities available to the Reichswehr, it was a natural progression that their interest in the Soviet Union moved away from economic penetration of the Soviet armament industry in favour of the expansion of the use and scope of military training facilities. Therefore, while many of the economic ventures were being run down, the use of training facilities was maintained and, in some instances expanded, after 1926. In January 1927 General Wetzell informed the Under Secretary of State to the Foreign Ministry that:

"The only German operations still functioning in the Soviet Union, ... were the following:

(1) the flying school at Lipetsk, which was a private enterprise supported by German government funds, (2) the tank school at Kazan, which was similarly organised (there were no active Reichswehr members employed on either, and the trainees were placed on inactive status), (3) some "scientific experiments with poison gas", in which Germany participated merely in an advisory capacity, and finally, (4) the yearly military missions to Russia's manoeuvres."[129]

Wetzell conceded that the first two operations were probably illegal under the Treaty of Versailles but argued that experience in tank and aerial warfare was vital:

"... these two weapons will play a decisive role in any future war."[130]

Although Stresemann was concerned by the political risks involved in the maintenance of these facilities, in February 1927, he agreed that the Reichswehr should continue to use its bases within the Soviet Union.[131]

The remaining doubts concerning the viability of the Russo-German military relationship seem to have centred on Moscow. Now that the benefits of German investment and technical expertise in Soviet industry were being gradually withdrawn, the direct returns from collaboration were largely restricted to co-operation in military training and organisation. Furthermore, the Scheidemann disclosures of December

1926 had been a major source of embarrassment to the Soviet government.[132]The western press had made capital out of the claim that the Soviet Union was in active co-operation with a bourgeois western government and could well have supplied the munitions used by the Reichswehr to suppress the communist uprising in Germany in 1923.[133] The Soviet leadership was also disturbed by Germany's decision to sign the Treaty of Locarno and subsequently to assume membership of the League of Nations. This appeared to indicate a growing identity of interests between Germany, France and Britain, perhaps ultimately aimed at the liquidation of communism.[134] Also, under Article 16 of the Covenant of the League of Nations, Germany could be required to allow armed forces to cross its territory if engaged in action designed to uphold the Covenant. To the Kremlin the possibility of western intervention in any future Russo-Polish conflict appeared all too real a prospect.[135]

However, although the Soviet leadership was concerned at the growing links that were apparently being established between Germany , France and Britain, it would seem that the value of the military ties with Germany were never seriously questioned. In a purely military context the value of the technical co-operation and training afforded to the Red Army at the German bases at Kazan and Lipetsk was inestimable. In addition, the experience gained by senior officers attending German army manoeuvres and staff officer training courses provided the groundwork for a complete revision of Red Army strategy and organisation. In a wider context, it was still considered that links between the Red Army and the Reichswehr provided the best prospect of securing German support, or at least benevolent neutrality, in the event of a further clash with Poland. [136]

It therefore appeared that the established military and potential political benefits derived from the military connections with Germany outweighed the comparative drawbacks. Within this analysis the lure of an alliance against Poland played a central role. However, while the possibility of such an alliance may have been well received and perhaps encouraged by Seeckt, in the post 1926 period it failed to take account of the reorientation of the domestic political balance, within Germany, away from the military hierarchy and back towards the elected government. Therefore, when in 1928 Colonel Werner von Blomberg, Chief of the German General Staff, visited the Soviet Union and was asked directly by the Commissar for War, Voroshilov, what Germany's reaction would be if Poland attacked the Soviet Union he could only reply that it was a:

"... matter of high policy for which the political authorities were alone responsible."[137]

A more direct example of restrictions being placed on the activity of the Reichswehr within the Soviet Union was provided by the debate surrounding the Soviet proposal first raised in October 1928, that Krupps build a factory for the production of high grade steel within the Soviet Union. The Reichswehr in their anxiety to foster Russo-German relations approved the scheme and pointed out that a re-buff would upset the delicate balance of the links already established. Dirksen, who had replaced Rantzau at the Moscow Embassy, supported this conclusion:

"It would certainly be a mistake, he warned, to consider the whole matter as merely an economic venture of concern only to German business. The Russians would always look upon it as a political matter, and it was "closely connected with our other operations here in the past. If we refuse to collaborate, our operations here will decline.".[138]

However, the scheme could only be sanctioned with the approval of the Foreign Ministry and although a tentative agreement was signed between the Soviet Union and Rheinmetall in February 1930 the refusal of the Foreign Ministry to fully back the programme effectively negated the possibility of it ever being put into operation.[139] This episode was symptomatic of the Reichswehr's continued preoccupation with the need for foreign training facilities and also a tacit understanding with the Soviet Union directed against Poland. It became increasingly apparent though, in the latter half of the 1920's that the Foreign Ministry was not prepared to take the risk of a Russo-German military alliance upsetting the delicate balance of relations with the western powers. Furthermore, although the military value of the bases in the Soviet Union was recognised, the German government refused to provide exorbitant aid to the Soviet economy merely to foster goodwill and political ties.

Whereas formerly the Reichswehr had taken the initiative in establishing the format of Russo-German relations it appeared that in the latter half of the decade the roles were reversed with the political relationship between the two nations increasingly dictating the format of the military links. The Reichswehr continued to use its bases within the Soviet Union until 1933 with great success in the development of tank and aerial warfare techniques.[140] However, during this period the political climate was in a state of flux. In the summer of 1932, in response to a suggestion that the German government had offered to conclude a military alliance with France, the Soviet leadership began to reassess its attitude towards Russo-German relations. To avoid the possibility of diplomatic and military isolation the Kremlin explored the potential for establishing alternative ties within Europe. The French Foreign Ministry saw the opportunity to weaken the Rapallo alignment and contain possible German expansionism in eastern Europe by responding to the Soviet overtures. The end product of this diplomatic activity was the Russo-French Non Aggression Pact signed in November 1932 which reinforced the Russo-Polish pact of July 1932.[141]

This move marked the first positive reorientation of Russo-German relations but it did not in itself impair the military relationship. However, in August 1932 a new factor was introduced onto the political scene with the accession of the National Socialist Party to power. Although previously the Soviet Union had accepted that it was possible to maintain ties with a regime that had violently suppressed domestic communism, the campaign of repression and harassment now mounted against not only the German Communist Party but also Soviet diplomatic, trade and press representatives within Germany was unparalleled.[142] In March 1933 Hitler reaffirmed that he wished to maintain cordial relations with the Soviet Union, but this apparent conciliatory gesture was not reflected in the growing press war being mounted between the two nations.

The German Foreign Minister, von Neurath, was concerned at the developing state of affairs. In March 1933 the German ambassador in Moscow had reported:

"... the development of Soviet-French relations will be correlated with that of German-Soviet relations: the greater the cooling towards Germany, the greater the disposition to cordiality toward France."[143]

Neurath appreciated the danger of pushing the Soviet Union into the French and Polish camps and on the basis of his fears in May 1933 the German police were instructed to take no further action against Soviet citizens without reference to the Foreign Ministry, while the National Socialist press was to moderate its anti-Communist line.[144]

However, these measures were too late to affect the train of events that had been set in motion. Although the protocol for the extension of the Treaty of Berlin was ratified in May 1933 in the summer of the same year the Soviet authorities demanded that the Reichswehr dismantle its bases within the Soviet Union.[145] This move was almost certainly inspired by political considerations as the advantages presented to both military forces from co-operation remained unaltered. The reorientation of Soviet foreign policy towards alliance with France and Poland had devalued the Russo-German relationship. In this sense military co-operation was but a pawn in the sphere of international diplomacy. In the autumn of 1933 all transportable equipment was shipped back to Germany while permanent fixtures were handed over to the Red Army. On September 19, 1933 the Military Attaché to the Moscow Embassy reported to the Foreign Ministry:

"The stations were discontinued on September 15. Therewith the period of many years of German-Russian military co-operation has been terminated in its previous form."[146]

On a purely military basis Russo-German military co-operation, which spanned a decade, was beneficial to both parties. In 1920 Seeckt had set out to rebuild the Reichswehr following the shattering blows dealt to it by the Versailles settlement. Twenty years later Major Wurmsiedler of the German General Staff acknowledged Seeckt's role in the creation of the modern Reichswehr by noting:

"When Hitler came to power in 1933 he found all the technical preparations for rearmament ready, thanks to the Reichswehr."[147]

This could only have been achieved by covertly circumventing the military and economic restrictions imposed on Germany after the war. Within this context the facilities provided for the use of the Reichswehr in the Soviet Union played a central role. At Lipetsk, which had a permanent staff of 150-200 German technical and flying officers disguised as the 4th Squadron of the Red Army, significant progress had been made in the development of modern metal aircraft and the training of aircrew in simulated combat conditions.[148] At Kazan similar advances had been made in tank design and strategy.[149] However, less was known of the poison gas centre at Torski except that extensive tests were undertaken on the military use of chlorine and phosgene.[150] The Red Army worked alongside the Reichswehr in all of these operations and was able to share in the developments in tank and aircraft design and the training of technical support staff. Furthermore, as a result of the staff officer training courses provided for senior Red Army officers in Berlin, the Soviet military machine underwent almost wholesale reform in terms of strategy and organisation.[151]

The Reichswehr was also active in promoting economic ties between the two nations. However, the amount of military material supplied by Soviet industry to the German army was virtually negligible and the goal of developing Soviet industry as a reservoir available to the German army was never achieved. Links were established, though, between German and Soviet industrialists that resulted in large orders being placed for German goods at a time of economic recession which permitted the Ruhr industrial complex to maintain its programme of technical development and the highly specialised work force that was required to man the projects. In return the Soviet Union received access to German goods, machinery and technical expertise which were invaluable in the rebuilding of its war-shattered economy.[152]

Therefore, in the military sphere, the Russo-German relationship appeared to have been constructed on the recognition of the benefits that could be mutually derived from co-operation. However, military links between the two nations was not complemented by co-operation between the Red Navy and the German Navy. The potential for co—operation seemed to exist in that the Germany Navy needed access to facilities for the construction and testing of weaponry forbidden by the Versailles treaty while the Red Navy had need of German technical expertise. In 1926 Soviet naval representatives visited Berlin on two occasions and offered to provide facilities for the construction of submarines and torpedoes in the Soviet Union as part of a joint project between the two countries.[153] The German Navy examined the project but declined the offer. This decision can be partially explained by the creation of German sponsored companies in Spain and Holland that were engaged in the manufacture of submarines ultimately destined for the German Navy. However in terms of strategy, it would seem that the navy was essentially preoccupied with the Atlantic and therefore in establishing an understanding with Britain. It was considered that the fringe benefits that would result from a Russo-German naval relationship did not warrant the political risk of damaging relations with Britain. The fact that links with the Soviet Union were considered of little value to the German navy was reflected by a naval study that concluded that access to Finnish raw material was potentially of more value than any prospective links with the Red Navy. The gulf between the attitudes adopted by the Reichswehr and the German naval authorities centred essentially on the field of strategy. While the German Navy looked essentially to the Atlantic and the North Sea, the attention of the Reichswehr focused primarily on Poland.[154] In their fear of Polish expansionism and their perception of the need to liquidate the Polish state, the Reichswehr and the Red Army shared a common bond that continually cemented their tacit alliance.

The basis of this relationship was firmly established during Seeckt's term of office as Chief of the Army High Command from the spring of 1920 until October 1926. Several leading German statesmen of the period, including Gustav Stresemann subsequently claimed that the programme had been initiated solely by the military authorities without the knowledge or approval of the German government. Although there were grounds for concluding that several highly placed politicians were not informed of the existence of covert military co-operation, the overwhelming mass of evidence indicated that the vast majority of senior government officials were aware of the nature of Reichswehr operations within the Soviet Union.[155] Although the political authorities were not prepared to risk the political consequences of a formal military alliance directed against Poland, they appreciated and approved of the practical military benefits produced by links with Soviet Union as a vital step in the neutralisation of the Versailles settlement. Furthermore, it was considered that the suggestion of some form of military understanding with the Soviet Union would strengthen the German hand in all aspects of relations with Poland, France and Britain. It would appear that the only major source of friction between the Reichswehr and the German government was concerned not with ultimate policy objectives but whether the programme should be directed by the Foreign Ministry or the Reichswehr.[156]

This problem was only solved in 1926 when, with the liquidation of many of the Reichswehr's economic projects within the Soviet Union, the administration of the remaining facilities was centralised in the Reichswehr's Moscow Headquarters which was effectively placed under the jurisdiction of the Moscow Embassy.

Yet, in essence, while the German army looked eastwards the politicians continued to gaze to the west.

For many the main benefit of the Rapallo agreement had been that it had forced France and Britain to consciously reassess their attitude towards Germany and perhaps to adopt a more conciliatory line. Guided by Gustav Stresemann and symbolised by the Treaty of Locarno, German foreign policy seemed to be aiming at a restoration of German prestige and influence in concert with the major powers of western Europe. It could, therefore, be suggested that the opening of Russo-German relations had been a consequence of German fear and suspicion of French ambitions. With the improvement of Franco-German relations after 1925 the Russo-German military links continually threatened to undermine the central westward orientation of German policy. However, to dismantle the relationship would not only have denied the Reichswehr access to invaluable training facilities but also threatened to weaken Germany's political and military situation by pushing the Soviet Union towards the French and Polish camp.[157] Therefore, during this period while the relationship did not significantly impair relations with the west, it was continued for it was perceived that the benefits derived from the links still outweighed the various drawbacks.

From the outset the Soviet leadership was equally pragmatic in its approach to the relationship. Lenin appreciated that the alliance was based on short term strategic goals:

> "When our ways part they (the Germans) will be our most ferocious and our great enemies. Time will tell whether a Germany hegemony or a Communist federation is to arise out of the ruins of Europe."[158]

While it had been the mutual distrust and hatred of Poland that had initially drawn the Reichswehr and the Red Army together it had also been considered that the aid rendered to the German re-armament programme was a paltry price to pay for German technical assistance in the rebuilding of the Soviet economy and military machine.[159] The Soviet government was prepared to minimise the ideological gulf between the two nations and ignore the suppression of the German communist movement in favour of a realistic outlook that appreciated the need for German assistance in the restoration of the Soviet state.

However, during the latter half of the decade political factors increasingly dictated the format of the military relationship. By 1933 no longer were Germany and the Soviet Union the political outcasts of Europe. Both nations were in the process of gradual reintegration into the international community. With the accession of the National Socialist Party to office in Germany a note of discord had now been introduced into the pattern of Russo-German relations. The outward indication of this discord was represented by the verbal war being conducted between the two nations through the medium of the press. Yet this in itself was not sufficient to explain the decision made by the Soviet government in the summer of 1933 to terminate all military links with Germany. This decision was based on the conclusion that Germany was no longer a reliable ally and indeed ideologically, presented a more immediate threat to Soviet security than the western capitalist states. In order to counter this threat the Soviet Union saw its interests as lying firmly with the European powers which favoured the maintenance of the status quo under the aegis of collective security. While, in the long term, this reorientation of policy was indicated by the Soviet Union's decision to join the League of Nations in September 1934,[160] the immediate product of this essentially defensive strategy was the pacts of non aggression concluded with Poland and France. These arrangements appeared to have effectively neutralised the Polish threat to Soviet security and established the potential for French assistance in the Soviet re-armament programme. Therefore, the two basic pillars upon which the Russo-German military relationship had been constructed seemed to have been undermined. In this context the value of links between the Reichswehr and the Red Army had to be reassessed. Hans Gatzke noted:

"There is no evidence that any of the civilian authorities were wholeheartedly in favour of the collaboration for military reasons alone."

"It was only when they became aware of the possible political or economic advantages that could be derived from the Reichswehr's Russian connections that the politicians became reconciled to, ..., such relations."[161]

However, now that the benefits derived from the Russo-German relationship were no longer indispensable long term political considerations dictated the format of future relations. Despite the creation of intimate military links, the civilian authorities in Moscow and Berlin appreciated that it could be no more than one strand of a temporary detente given the strategic and ideological chasm that s separated the two nations.[162] Military connections between Germany and the Soviet Union had not been accompanied by a coalescence of political interests. Therefore, it was only natural that in the long term the military relationship would be sacrificed to the higher interests of national security and political strategy. Gatzke observed:

"Their collaboration did not amount to a conspiracy, not because they had any aversion to it but because they knew that a conspiracy presupposes mutual trust between conspirators. Germany's political leaders realised, as their military colleagues did not, that it was impossible to have such trust in a government whose aims threatened the very existence of friend and foe alike."[163]

References

1. John W Wheeler-Bennett, **The Nemesis of Power The German Army in Politics, 1918-1945** (London, 1967, p 31.

2. The orderly withdrawal of the German Army from the western front gave rise to the belief that the army had not been defeated in battle but had been betrayed by the politicians. The falsity of such a view is revealed by a note from Field Marshal Hindenburg to Prince Max von Baden dated October 3, 1918:

   "The Supreme Command insists on its demand of Sunday 29 September, that a peace offer to our enemies be issued at once.

As a result of the collapse of the Macedonian front and the weakening of our Western reserves which this has brought about, and now that it is impossible to make good the very considerable losses which have been incurred in the battles of the last few days, there is, so as can be foreseen, no longer a prospect of Forcing peace on the enemy.

The enemy, on the other hand, is continually bringing new and fresh reserves into the battle. The German army still stands firm and successfully wards of all attacks. But the situation may force the Supreme Command to take momentous decisions.

It is desirable in the circumstances to break off the battle in order to spare the German people and its allies useless sacrifices. Every day wasted costs thousands of brave soldiers their lives."

Prince Max von Baden, **The Memoirs of Prince Max of Baden Volume II** (London, 1928), p 19.

3. It is not the purpose of this chapter to delve too deeply into the concept of the Prussian military tradition. However, Dr H Ebeling attempted to define it in the following terms:

"Prussianism: This means something which originated and grew up on the soil of Prussia, the dynastic state with its rigid orders of society. And it was the character of this state which moulded the character of the Prussian and prussianised German armies and their officer corps.

Militarism: This means the achievement of political independence by the army and the officers corps. The exaltation of the man who wears the "King's uniform" above the ordinary civilian, the elevation of the professional officer to the first rank of state. The army for the army's sake. Civil life and the state of the peace usually associated with it - and, consequently, policy and national economy - are solely directed towards was, towards war for the sake of the army."

Dr H Ebeling, **The Caste. The Political Role of the German General Staff between 1918 and 1938**, (London, 1945), p 5.

Although this, in essence, is an oversimplification of the concept it does indicate the basic nature of Prussian militarism. For a more detailed analysis of the topic see Gordon A Craig, **The Politics of the Prussian Army**, 1640-1945 (London, 1964).

4. Gordon A Craig, **The Politics of the Prussian Army,1640-1945** (London, 1964), p 393.

5. F L Carsten, **The Reichswehr and Politics, 1918-1933** (London, 1966), p 50-51.

6. These right wing elements were based essentially on the Freikorps formations that were legalised by the German government on January 9, 1919 ostensibly to defend the nation against the internal and external threat generated by the Bolshevik revolution. However Wheeler-Bennett concluded:

"The Free Corps, though nominally for the defence of the Reich within and without, became a potential

weapon for the active preservation of militant and reactionary nationalism ..."

John W Wheeler-Bennett, **The Nemesis of Power**, p 42.

It was elements of the Freikorps led by General von Luttwitz that formed the cornerstone of the Kapp Putsch.

7. E H Carr, **German-Soviet relations between the two World Wars, 1919-1939** (Baltimore, 1967) p 28-29.

8. For a wider discussion of the role of the German General Staff during the First World War see Martin Kitchen, **The Silent Dictatorship** (London, 1976).

9. Carsten, op cit p 78-89.

10. Wheeler-Bennett, op cit p 83-87.

11. Colonel General von Seeckt, **Royal United Services Institute, LXXII, No 485 (February 1927)**, p 174-176.

12. Carsten, op cit p 42-43.

13. Wheeler-Bennett, op cit p 83-86.

14. Carsten, op cit p 79.

15. Craig, op cit p 377.

16. G W F Hallgarten, **General Hans von Seeckt and Russia, 1920-1922**, Journal of Modern History No 21 (March, 1949), p 28-34 At p 28.

17. Wheeler-Bennett, op cit p 86-87.

18. Ibid., p 86.

19. Alistair Horne, **To Lose a Battle. France 1940** (London, 1969), p 39.

20. Craig, op cit. p 385.

21. Wheeler-Bennett, op cit. p 90.

22. Ibid., 10C cit.

23. Ibid., p 88.

24. Craig. op cit. p 388.

25. Wheeler-Bennett, op cit. p 87.

26. Ibid., 10C cit.

27. Ibid., p 95.

28. Craig. op cit. p 388-389.

29. Wheeler-Bennett, op cit. p 102-119.

30. Ibid., p 118-119.

31. Craig, op cit. p 392.

32. Horne, op cit. p 40. See also Rosinski, **The German Army** (Washington, 1944).

33. Wheeler-Bennett, op cit. p 143.34

34. Horne, op cit. p 40.

35. General von Seeckt, **Modern Armies, Royal United Services Institute, LXXIV, No 493** (February 1929), p 123-131.

36. Horne, op cit. p 40.

37. Craig, op cit. p 397.

38. Major-General J F C Fuller (C I C Tank Corps) conceived his "plan 1919" which involved three forces of tanks. A disorganising force of fast mediums to break straight through the front-line trenches and attack the enemy's divisional corps and army headquarters in the first two hours of any attack; a "breaking force" to be thrown against the main front as soon as the brains of the enemy command were disorganised; and a "pursuing force" of mediums accompanied by lorried infantry to follow through the gap to "mop up" the enemy's rear areas. The design of the "medium D" tank was well advanced in late 1918 so the feasibility of such a plan was not in doubt.

It can be argued, therefore, that Fuller had invented the "Blitzkreig" tactic of warfare. These ideas were given wide circulation in May 1920 when it was announced that Fuller had won the gold medal for the prize essay in the Military Essay Competition of the Royal United Services Institution (RUSI) and had opened his essay with the following words:

"War is a matter of tools, and the highest mechanical weapon nearly always wins... Had Napoleon had a company of machine-guns at Waterloo, he would have won that battle; had we, in 1914 had tanks we should have won this war the same year ... The change in the art of war effected by the introduction of the petrol engine on the battlefield has been stupendous, for it has opened up a new epoch in the history of war to which we can find no parallel in land fighting, the nearest approach being the

*replacement of sails by steam as the motive means in naval warfare ..." *1*

An early disciple of Fuller's original concepts of mechanised warfare was Captain B H Liddell Hart who by the end of the 1920's was the foremost tactical theorist in the mechanised sphere of warfare.

In 1929 Liddell Hart published two of the most important works on strategy and tactics of the interwar years. His seminal biography and study of William Tecumsah Sherman and "The Decisive Wars of History". In "Sherman" Hart saw that Sherman's and Nathan Bedford Forrest's campaigns behind the enemy lines and their raiding tactics which cut the communications and supply lines of forces who were relying on railway communications, contained lessons which were of tremendous potential in the 1930's:

*"... in (Sherman) I saw particularly the value of unexpectedness as the best guarantee of security as well as of rapid progress; the value of flexibility in plan and dispositions, above all by operating on a line which offers and threatens alternative objectives (thus, in Sherman's phrase, putting the opponent, on 'the horns of a dilemma'); the value of what I termed the 'baited gambit' to trap the opponent, by combining offensive strategy with defensive tactics, or elastic defence with well-timed riposte; the need to cut down the load of equipment and other impedimenta - as Sherman did - in order to develop mobility and flexibility." *2*

Using his study of Sherman and Forrest as a base, Liddell Hart thus developed the theory of the "expanding torrent" method of attack with mechanised forces, which tactics he had worked out in 1920 into a strategy which was to prove invaluable to the Germans via Guderian:

"The secret lies partly in the tactical combination of tanks and aircraft, partly in the unexpectedness of the stroke in direction and time, but above all in the follow through - the exploitation of a breakthrough (the tactical penetration of a front) into a deep strategic penetration, carried out by armoured forces racing on ahead of the main army and operating independently.

The pace of such forces promises a decisively deep penetration so long as it can be kept up. It is kept up by a torrent-like process of advance, either swerving round resistance or piercing it at a weakened spot - in which case the tank-torrent contracts in pouring through a narrow breach, and then expands again to its original breadth.

It is the persistent pace, coupled with the variability of the thrustpoint that paralyses the opponent. For at every stage, after the original break-through, the flexible drive of the armoured forces carries simultaneously several alternative threats, while the threat which actually develops into a thrust takes place too quickly for the enemy's reserve to reach the spot in time to stiffen the resistance there before it collapses. In effect, both tactical and strategical *surprise are maintained from start to finish. It is a high-speed 'indirect approach' to the enemy's rear areas - where his vital and vulnerable organs of control and supply are located." *3*

*1 Quoted in B H Liddell Hart **"Memoirs" Volume I** Cassell, London 1965 Pages 88-89.

*2 ibid page 166.

*3 B H Liddell Hart **"The Tanks: the History of the Royal Tank Regiment and its Predecessors"** Volume II Cassell, London 1959 Pages 453-454.

39. Horne op cit. p 41-43. See also Kenneth Macksey. **Guderian Panzer General** (London, 1975) and **General Heinz Guderian, Panzer Leader** (London,, 1974).

40. Wheeler-Bennett, op cit. p 92-98.

41. Ibid., p 119-120.

42. G Hilger and A Meyer **The Incompatible Allies** (New York, 1953) p 191.

43. Wheeler-Bennett, op cit. p 119-120.

44. F L Carsten. **The Reichswehr and the Red Army, 1920-1933**, Survey, October 1962, p 114-132, at p 16.

45. A L Smith, **The German General Staff and Russia, 1919-1926**, Soviet Studies, October 1956, p 125-132, at p 125-126.

46. Carsten, **The Reichswehr and the Red Army**, p 115.

47. Ibid., p 116.

48. G A Craig and F Gilbert, **The Diplomats 1919-1939 Volume I The Twenties** (New York, 1972) p 167-168.

49. Smith, op cit. p 127.

50. Carr, op cit. p 14-16.

51. Macksey, op cit. p 25-34.

52. Craig, op cit. p 168.

53. Carsten, **The Reichswehr and the Red Army**, p 117. See also Carr, p 17-24 and Gustav Hilger and Alfred Meyer, **The Incompatible Allies. A Memoir History of German-Soviet Relations 1918-1941** (New York, 1953) p 191.

54. Lionel Kochan, **Russia and the Weimar Republic** (Cambridge, 1954) P 16-17.

55. Wheeler-Bennett, op cit. p 125.

56. Ibid., p 124-125.

57. Carr, op cit. p 23-24.

58. Carsten, **The Reichswehr and the Red Army**, p 117.

59. Kochan, op cit. p 35-41.

60. Carsten, **The Reichswehr and the Red Army**, p 117.

61. Kochan, op cit. p 36.

62. Gilbert and Craig, op cit. p 246-264.

63. Kochan, op cit. p 38-39.

64. Ibid., p 38.

65. Wheeler-Bennett, op cit. p 126-127.

66. Carr, op cit. p 47.

67. Ibid., p 47.

68. Kochan, op cit. p 41. See also Carr, p 38-39.

69. Wheeler-Bennett, op cit. p 127. See also Craig, p 409.

70. Kochan, op cit. p 60.

71. Smith, op cit. p 128.

72. Hilger and Meyer, op cit. p 194-196. Also Craig, op cit. p 409.

73. Hallgarten, op cit. p 30. Also Carsten op cit. p 118-119.

74. Smith op cit. p128.

75. Ibid., p 129.

76. Craig, op cit. p 410-411.

77. Hallgarten, op cit. p 32.

78. Carsten, **The Reichswehr and the Red Army**, op cit. p 120.

79. Huger and Meyer, op cit. p 193.

80. Smith, op cit. p 129.

81. Hilger and Meyer,j op cit. p 205.

82. Hallgarten, op cit. p 31.

83. Carr, op cit. p 60.

84. Kochen, op cit. p 62.

85. Ibid., p 62-63.

86. Wheeler-Bennett, op cit. p 132.

87. Craig, op cit. p 411.

88. Wheeler-Bennett,~ op cit. p137.   -

89. Ibid., 10C cit.

90. Ibid., p 138.

91. Gerald Freund, **Unholy Alliance. Russian-German Relations from the Treaty of Brest-Litovsk to the Treaty of Berlin** (London, 1957), p 202.

92. Carsten, **The Reichswehr and the Red Army**, op cit. p 120.

93. Hilger and Meyer, op cit. p 196-197.

94. Hans W Gatzke, Russo-German Military Collaboration during the Weimar Republic. Taken from Hans W Gatzke (ED), **European Diplomacy between Two Wars**, 1919-1939 (Chicago, 1972), p 44.

95. Ibid., p 45.

96. Hilger and Meyer, op cit. p 200-201.

97. Gatzke, op cit. p 46.

98. Freund, op cit. p 203.

99. Gatzke, op cit. p 47-48.

100. Ibid., p 49.

101. Ibid., 10C cit.

102. Ibid., p 50.

103. Carsten, **The Reichswehr and the Red Army**, op cit. p 121-122.

104. Freund, op cit. p 205-210.

105. Ibid., IOC cit.

106. P Chamberlain and C Ellis, **Tanks of the World, 1915-1945** (London, 1972) See pages 43, 47 and 210.

107. Wheeler-Bennett, op cit. p 150-153.

108. As Colonel von Stulpnagel noted following Seeckt's resignation in 1926:

> *"The affair of the prince only played a minor part, although it was the straw which broke the camel's back."*

In essence the affair was indicative of the growing conflict between Seeckt and the leading political figures of the Weimar regime. While Seeckt's personal authority and position were unchallenged during the early years of the Weimar government the election of Field-Marshal Paul von Hindenburg to the post of President in April 1925 effectively reorganised the balance of power. The fact that only one senior German Staff Officer apparently urged Seeckt to resist dismissal indicated that Hindenburg had largely superseded Seeckt as the focus of Reichswehr loyalty. F L Carsten concluded:

> *"Thus no gap was created by Seeckt's dismissal in the relations between the officer corps and the head of state. On the contrary, as the Reichswehr could hardly be loyal to two "royal substitutes" at the same*

time Seeckt's disappearance was the logical outcome of the election of the new president. Seeckt's dismissal did not create an upheaval: it passed almost unnoticed."

See F L Carsten **The Reichswehr in Politics 1918— 1933** (London, 1969) p 245-250.

109. Hilger and Meyer, op cit. p 201.

110. Freund, op cit. p 210-211.

111. Hiluger and Meyer, op cit. p 202.

112. Carsten, **The Reichswehr and Politics**, op cit. p 234.

113. Freund, op cit. p 211-212.

114. Craig, op cit. p 424 and Hallgarten, op cit. p 30-31.

115. Carr, op cit. p 94-95.

116. Ibid., p 95.

117. Wheeler-Bennett, op cit. p 107.

118. Ibid., p 141.

119. Freund, op cit. p 204-205.

120. Wheeler-Bennett, op cit. p 140-141.

121. Carsten, **The Reichswehr and the Red.Army**, op cit. p 125.

122. Ibid., 10C cit.

123. Hilger and Meyer, op cit. p 205-206.

124. Ibid., p 206.

125. Gatzke, op cit. p 55.

126. Wheeler-Bennett, op cit. p 145.

127. Ibid., p 146.

128. Craig. op cit. p 406.

129. Gatzke op cit. p 56.

130. Ibid., 10C cit.

131. Ibid., p 57-58 also Hilger and Meyer, op cit. p 206-207.

132. Carsten, **The Reichswehr and the Red Army**, op cit. p 126.

133. Hilger and Meyer, op cit. p 204.

134. Kochan, op cit. p 99-102.

135. Craig and Gilbert, op cit. p 171.

136. Gatzke, op cit. p 58.

137. Ibid., 10C cit.

138. Ibid., p 59.

139. Ibid., p59-62.

140. Horne, op cit. p 39-43.

141. G H Stein, **Russo-German Military Collaboration. The Last Phase, 1933**, Political Science Quarterly, LXXVII, March 1949, p 54-71, at p 54-57.

142. Ibid., p60.

143. Ibid., p59.

144. Ibid., p62-63.

145. Ibid., p66.

146. Ibid., p 54.

147. Wheeler-Bennett, op cit. p 148.

148. Freund, op cit. p 206-210.

149. Carsten, **The Reichswehr and the Red Army**, op cit. p 124-125.

150. Ibid., op cit. p 122.

151. Hilger and Meyer, op cit. p 198.

152. Smith, op cit. p 131-132.

153. Carsten, **The Reichswehr and the Red Army**, op cit. p 127.

154. Ibid., p 128-130.

155. Freund, p 202-203 also Gatzke,~ op cit. p 64.

156. Freund, op cit. p 201.

157. Gatzke, op cit. p 64.

158. Wheeler-Bennett, op cit. p 127.

159. Gatzke, op cit. p 65.

160. F P Walters, **A History of the League of Nations** London, 1969), p 579-585.

161. Gatzke, op cit. p 64.

162. Stein, op cit. p 71.

163. Gatzke, op cit. p 65.